THE GREAT LIVES SERIES

Great Lives biographies shed an exciting new light on the many dynamic men and women whose actions, visions, and dedication to an ideal have influenced the course of history. Their ambitions, dreams, successes and failures, the controversies they faced and the obstacles they overcame are the true stories behind these distinguished world leaders, explorers, and great Americans.

Other biographies in the Great Lives Series

A special thanks to educators Dr. Frank Moretti, Ph.D., Associate Headmaster of the Dalton School in New York City; Dr. Paul Mattingly, Ph.D., Professor of History at New York University; and Barbara Smith, M.S., Assistant Superintendent of the Los Angeles Unified School District, for their contributions to the Great Lives Series.

GREAT LIVES

CLARA BARTON
Founder of the American Red Cross

Susan Sloate

FAWCETT COLUMBINE
NEW YORK

TABLE OF CONTENTS

Clara Barton during her years as a school teacher.

1

Under Fire

THE SMOKE HANGING over the Virginia cornfield blocked out the sights, but not the sounds, of battle. While soldiers choked in the fog, they could hear the screams of horses, the clatter of hooves, the firing of cannons, and the groans of their dying comrades.

It was September, 1862, and Union and Confederate forces were fighting the Civil War. The Second Battle of Bull Run, in Manassas, Virginia, had been won by the Confederate Army and the Union troops had been forced to make a hasty retreat. On their way, however, they met with "Stonewall" Jackson's Confederate forces near a tiny Virginia town. Now, with one battle barely ended, the Battle of Chantilly was underway.

As soldiers fell on the battlefield, the other soldiers slung them onto rough wagons and carried them the two miles to the Fairfax train station, which had been quickly set up as a field hospital. There they were dumped on floors with thousands of other wounded men, faces blackened, arms and legs bleeding, some al-

1

ready dying, to wait their turn for attention from the overworked surgeons.

The surgeons were working swiftly, but their job was endless. There were only a few doctors to tend to three thousand wounded, and they were rapidly using up what little medical supplies they had. They could not leave their medical duties to feed the soldiers, and no one had offered the wounded men either food or water since they'd been brought in. Left alone, soldiers died of thirst and neglect as swiftly as they succumbed to their wounds. A cloud of despair settled over the farmhouse, a cloud as thick as the smoke of battle outside.

Suddenly, a petite woman in simple black skirts topped by a tiny red bow marched into the station, trailed by two female assistants. Her arms were piled high with fresh bandages and supplies. Behind her stood a train loaded with boxes and barrels, containing every comfort she could round up to ease the suffering of the wounded.

This courageous woman, a former schoolteacher and government clerk was Clara Barton. She was the first woman to serve the wounded at actual battle sites, instead of in faraway field hospitals. Through the four years of the American Civil War, she would slog through miles of mud and rain, sleep on boxes in tents, work through long days and nights of broiling sun and bitter cold, feeding, sheltering, and nursing both Union and Confederate soldiers wounded in battle. For her extraordinary service — the first of its kind ever done by a woman — she was hailed by the soldiers as the "Angel of the Battlefield."

Now the surgeons at Chantilly looked at her, amazed.

She stood just five feet tall, in a plain black dress that covered her ankles. She was forty years old, with a strong face, clear, compassionate brown eyes, and a ready smile. Often, in the heat of her work with the wounded, she pinned up her skirts to form a large apron and rolled up her sleeves. She was certainly an odd-looking figure, though she was graceful and swift on her feet.

The doctors welcomed her with open arms. Despite the fact that she had been nursing at the Second Battle of Bull Run only two days before, Clara looked as serene, alert and energetic as any soldier marching off to battle. With the doctors' supplies dwindling to almost nothing, her offer of fresh linen, food and dressings must have seemed like something out of a dream. As soon as her arms were empty, she turned to the soldiers to decide how best to help. In just a few minutes, she and her assistants were breaking open boxes of supplies and boiling cornmeal in a large kettle. They stuffed their pockets with crackers, dipped bread in wine to restore strength to the wounded, and set off to feed each man where he lay.

Clara herself worked for four days without sleep or food. When she had no more cornmeal, she made a thick drink out of wine, water, crushed army biscuits, and brown sugar, but she discovered there were almost no bowls, plates, or dishes to serve it in. Immediately, she gave orders to her assistants to help her empty wine bottles and jelly jars, which they then filled with the drink and held for the tired men to sip. When that gave out, they took the meat filling intended for their own sandwiches and gave that to the wounded.

When she had fed the soldiers as well as possible, Clara began to walk about with clean linen and clothing. She bandaged minor wounds in soft cloth and sponged off sweaty, grimy faces. One soldier, shivering in a rag of a shirt, attracted her notice. As she moved closer to cover his chest, he threw an arm around her neck and began to cry.

Startled, Clara looked into his face and recognized the face of one of her first students in a small Massachusetts school, many years before. He was one of the boys who had waited for her after school to carry home her books — but the arm that used to carry them now lay at his side, shattered and useless. It would never carry any more books. Quietly, she tucked the edges of his shirt around him and went on her way.

Hours later, one of the surgeons stopped her. Lying up on the hillside was a young boy, probably dying, who kept calling for his sister Mary. He was disturbing the other soldiers and refused to try to sleep until his sister came to him.

Clara followed the surgeons to the boy, and in the darkness she sank to the ground, took his hand and kissed his forehead. The boy cried out, sure that she was his sister. Then he finally allowed himself to fall asleep, while Clara sat with him, cradling his cold body until he began to grow warm again.

At dawn the boy opened his eyes, now clear and calm, and saw Clara sitting next to him. "I know now she couldn't get here," he said, puzzled. "But who are you?"

"Just a woman who came to help you," Clara told him. With that she rose, and went at once to the sur-

4

geons to beg them to help him as soon as possible. As a result, the boy lived long enough to return to Washington and die in the arms of his beloved sister Mary.

Another pressing problem, Clara noticed, was the care of the wounded who were loaded onto ambulances. The ambulances themselves were horrible, shaky carts that jounced the men about, making them suffer even more and often killing them before they could reach Washington.

Worse, no one checked the wounded to be sure they were given food and water before the ambulances started the eight-mile journey to Washington. Men who had otherwise minor wounds died of hunger and thirst simply because there was no system to keep track of who had been fed and who had not.

Clara went to the officers in charge and insisted that each cart line up before setting off, so that she and her assistants could feed the soldiers. The officers finally agreed, and Clara climbed into ambulances and fed the men herself, kneeling beside them while they ate and drank. It was a crude assembly line, but a vital one, and Clara felt satisfied as the ambulances rumbled off, that at least the men had been given enough food to help them survive the long trip back to the capital.

As nightfall came, thousands of soldiers still lay in and around Fairfax Station. The lucky ones had makeshift beds of hay, on which they stretched out, but the darkness brought yet another problem. Clara and her workers had only candles with which to see while they worked, and everywhere they turned more wounded men lay. With every move they risked stepping on a body — and even worse was the danger of a fire, should

5

any candles be dropped. One candle touching a piece of straw could be a disaster, since there was no way to move the men out of the way.

Fortunately, as they waited, worked and prayed, the candles remained upright. The women moved gently among the men, until they gave out in sheer exhaustion. Her assistants went off for a nap while Clara worked on doggedly. At last she too stopped — but there was no place in her tiny, crowded tent to lie down. One assistant slept on top of the only box in the tent, and rain was pouring down outside. Clara crawled into a small waterlogged space, and despite the wet, slept for two hours. When she awoke, she wrung out her drenched hair and skirt and went back to work.

Federal trains were pulling into the station to transport the wounded to Washington, as the Confederates fought their way closer and closer. As Clara and the two women scrubbed, bandaged and cooked, they could hear the gunfire. They had few supplies left now, having given everything they brought with them to the soldiers. All they could do at this point was see to the loading of the wounded on the trains and offer a sip of water before they set off.

Suddenly, a Union officer rode through the mass of wounded calling for Clara. He told her the Confederates were going to overpower the Union forces, and if they smashed through soon, she might be taken prisoner. He told her to leave right away.

Clara sent her assistants off at once, but she remained. The officer warned her that staying might mean riding a horse cross-country in order to escape. He had no lady's saddle. Could she ride his?

6

"Yes," Clara told him confidently. "Or without it." As a child she had ridden wild horses bareback and felt comfortable on any kind of horse now.

The officer was relieved. "Then you can risk another hour here," he said. He promised to return shortly.

Clara doubled her efforts and watched as the last wounded man on the hillside was piled into the train for Washington. Soon, though, as she looked behind her, the Confederate army, in gray and butternut, poured down the hillside.

The Union officer who had come before rode up now at top speed. "Get on the train," he urged her. "Or you'll have to risk an escape cross-country."

Clara snatched up the few remaining supplies and hurried to get aboard the train pulling out of Fairfax Station. In a few minutes, as she watched, the Confederates burned the station to the ground. Nothing was left of the shelter where she and her assistants had given so much aid to so many.

Throughout her remarkable life, Clara Barton served in many capacities to relieve ignorance, pain, and every kind of suffering. As a young woman, she taught in schools, bringing calm and discipline to students who had never known either. She went into government service at a time when few women were even allowed to visit offices, let alone work there. When the Civil War began, she refused to remain in the safety behind the lines and insisted on meeting the emergencies on the battlefield.

After the war, Clara's greatest battles began — on behalf of an organization known as the American Red Cross. When others refused to support it, Clara herself took responsibility for building it up, bringing it to the attention of three different presidents, and finally seeing it supported by the United States government.

Even then her battles did not end. Rival organizations seeking to steal its glory sprang up around the Red Cross, only to be defeated by Clara's perseverance and determination. Other rivals within the Red Cross tried to blacken her name in order to force her to resign her position as the first president of the organization.

Clara, however, remained steadfast in her pursuit of the dream — a group of people who would always be available in times of emergency to assist, rebuild, and encourage people to help themselves. She won that fight, but at a terrible price to herself.

It was characteristic of Clara that her battles were all fought on behalf of other people. Despite her strength and optimism, she almost never fought a battle for herself. She was sensitive to criticism and easily wounded by gossip, but she did not waste her time defending herself. She had a larger job to do, and she felt that job came first. Even though that job would take nearly the rest of her life, she never turned away from it. When she was through, her contribution would stand as one of the greatest achievements in American history.

2

Growing Up Shy

F OR SOME PEOPLE, their adult lives are determined partly by the struggles they face as children. The demons that terrify them in their early years often haunt them throughout their lives. This was very much the case with Clara Barton.

North Oxford, Massachusetts was a farming community in 1821. In spring the fields were green with vegetables, and the winters were bitter cold. Families were large, since many hands were needed to tend the crops. A new baby was always welcome.

On Christmas Day, 1821, Sarah and Stephen Barton welcomed their first new baby in ten years. She was a dark-eyed child whom they named Clarissa Harlowe Barton, after an aunt who in turn was named for a popular literary heroine of her time. The name Clarissa was too long and frilly, however, for a practical little girl in a farming family. As she grew up, she simply called herself Clara.

Clara's parents came from strong Massachusetts blood. Her mother, the former Sarah Stone, came from a family whose ancestors had fought the British during the American Revolution. Her father Stephen, a former cavalry captain with General "Mad" Anthony Wayne, had fought Indians before settling down in North Oxford as a farmer and community leader.

Clara was a busy child who often dressed in deep red, her favorite color. Besides her love for her father's wild horses, she also adored the company of her kitten Button, who sometimes even slept with her in her little bed.

The Barton children, all much older than Clara, were delighted to have a little sister. Now they could teach her what each of them loved best. Her eldest brother Stephen Jr., a sturdy, handsome boy, taught her arithmetic as soon as she began to talk. Her next brother, David, threw her on the back of a wild colt when she was five and told her to hang on to the horse's mane. Soon he had her galloping all over the farm, laughing with delight. David's lessons gave Clara a lifetime pleasure in riding and equipped her to face an emergency in which the ability to ride any horse could save her life. David also taught his little sister carpentry, and Clara was soon able to use a hammer and saw, which came in handy later in her life.

Her sister Dorothea (nicknamed Dolly) was a schoolteacher, and though she had occasional fits of depression, she tutored Clara in reading and writing. Sally, the nearest to Clara in age, was ten years old when Clara was born. She also planned to teach school when she grew up, so she learned her profession by helping Dolly with the lessons.

Clara's mother Sarah made sure her youngest daughter knew how to keep house and cook, which she knew would be important when Clara ran a household of her own. She could not foresee that Clara would use these lessons in preserving fruits and sewing curtains on the battlefield and during various disasters. However, without her mother's lessons, Clara could never have been as effective as she later became. She admired and respected her mother's practicality and common sense, and as she grew older, she leaned more and more to the practical side of every problem.

Clara's father Stephen taught her her very favorite lessons of all. In spinning stories for her of his days fighting Indians, he explained to her the basics of military strategy. He and Clara used kernels of corn as soldiers in the mock battles they played out on the floor of the Barton home. Years later, Clara remarked of her army experiences, "Generals, colonels, captains and sergeants were given their proper place and rank. I never addressed a colonel as captain, got my cavalry on foot or mounted my infantry." She credited all of this to the patient teachings of her father in the military games they played together.

Since all of her teachers were many years older than she, Clara spent much of her time trying to perform tasks at a higher level than that normally expected of a very young child. She was learning from brothers and sisters who expected her to read, ride, and use a hammer as well as they did. If she could not or did not, she began to think they would not love her.

This mistaken belief gave birth, in little Clara, to a fierce need for excellence. As the youngest child, she desperately needed the love of her brothers and sisters, and she felt that achievement was the only way in which she could win that love. Therefore, it became important to do everything as well as she possibly could.

This combined need for excellence and fear of scorn led to Clara's toughest problem. Though she was remarkably courageous in riding wild ponies and crossing narrow footbridges, her early exposure to the criticism of her brothers and sisters led her to fear the criticism of others.

This, in turn, led her to dread even friendly contact with others. She was petrified of strangers. The sight of strange children could reduce her to tears, and she dreaded any contact with anyone she had not known since babyhood. When a stranger asked to meet her, she became speechless. She often awoke in the middle of the night, crying with terror over her dreams.

Clara's family, not realizing where her fears had come from, believed she would grow out of them. They refused to baby her or shelter her. They were strong, hardy people, and they insisted that Clara become strong and hardy as well. To teach her self-reliance, they enrolled her in a small one-room school in North Oxford before her fourth birthday.

Her oldest brother Stephen carried her on his shoulder through the silent white of a Massachusetts snowstorm to her first day at school. The tiny child was numb with terror. At the threshold of the bare wooden room, she faced her new teacher, Richard Stone, a kind and handsome man with children of his own, as well as the curious eyes of her new classmates.

Stone invited the little girl to sit down at one of the desks. She was unable to move or take her eyes off him.

Quietly, he set about easing her fears. He opened a spelling book and asked her whether she could read the word printed there. It was the word "cat."

Clara lifted her tiny head proudly. "I don't spell there," she informed him.

"Oh? Where do you spell?"

"I spell in artichoke," she answered. Clara meant that she could spell long words, words of three syllables, and "artichoke" was the first such word listed in her spelling book. Her sisters' reading lessons had helped her over the first hurdle. Despite her paralyzing shyness, she was pleased to do something well, and Mr. Stone, recognizing this pride as an asset in helping her, moved her up at once to a third-grade level reading class.

From the very beginning of her school career, Clara's grades were excellent, since she had so many teachers and critics at home. She herself once said that she had no brothers and sisters, but rather "six fathers and mothers" to watch over her as she grew.

None of the "six fathers and mothers" was very happy, however, when Clara's shyness continued. Instead of going away as her confidence grew, the shyness stayed stubbornly with her. Clara led her class in academics but could not bring herself to make friends with her schoolmates.

For several years she attended the little North Oxford schoolhouse, yet even when her own sisters taught there, Clara could not relax. Her continuous fear of strangers controlled her life.

Captain and Mrs. Barton believed they could cure her shyness by sending her to boarding school when she

13

was eight years old. They chose a school some distance away run by Richard Stone, Clara's first teacher. Though she remembered and loved him, Clara was heartsick at the new school, which was far from North Oxford and her family. She continued to do well in her schoolwork, but she was always terrified that she would do something wrong and make her classmates laugh at her. She made no friends, slept poorly, and was hardly able to eat anything.

The result was that her parents finally had to withdraw Clara from Mr. Stone's school. From then on she studied at home. When her brothers and sisters were not working with her, she worked happily with tutors hired to teach her specific subjects. Her interest in learning remained sharp, but she no longer suffered from the heartache of being thrown in with strangers.

The Barton fortune, however, played a role in helping Clara begin to overcome her fears. About the time Clara was eight, Jeremiah Learned, Captain Barton's nephew, died after a long illness. His wife and four children had depleted their financial reserves in caring for him, and they had almost nothing left to run their farm.

Captain Barton bought the Learned farm and moved his wife and Clara in with Mrs. Learned and her growing children. Stephen and David, now grown men, remained back at the Barton farm to manage it, and Dolly and Sally stayed with them to run the household. For the first time, Clara was living with children her own age. From the beginning, she loved it.

Being a child in a household full of children restored Clara's confidence. She was no longer competing with the older, bigger, stronger children, but simply enjoying herself. With her cousins, she roamed the farm, played hide and seek, scampered over rotted log bridges, experimented with ice-skating. She remained shy with strangers, but she was no longer the terrified child who woke screaming from nightmares. She was finally permitted to do things at her own level, and the change in her was remarkable.

However, the feeling that she needed to earn her family's love would always remain with Clara. The first hint of her later life — and her way of dealing with that need — surfaced in 1833, when she was eleven years old.

Her brother, David, whom she adored, fell off the roof while he and some friends were building a barn. He was very ill, and the doctors were worried that he might not live. Clara was grief-stricken, and afraid. She could not sit by and do nothing. Instead, she volunteered to nurse him.

From the beginning, she astonished her family and the community by her immediate understanding of nursing. Though still tiny for her age, she was strong enough to turn David in his bed, gentle enough to feed and bathe him without aggravating his injuries, and cheerful enough to keep up his spirits during his long confinement.

David was bedridden for two years and in dangerous condition for much of that time. Part of the reason, ironically, was the doctors' methods of treating him. At the time, the great medical cure-all was the use of leeches, large blood-sucking worms. In Clara's day, doctors believed that "bleeding" patients by letting leeches suck their blood would help them recover from many different types of illnesses. Doctors would apply the leeches over portions of the patient's body and let them suck all the blood they could hold. When they could suck no more, they fell off. Patients were bled for every kind of sickness, including headaches, fevers, measles, and broken bones.

David, the doctors decided, needed daily sessions with the leeches. This decision, more than any other, was the one that almost killed him. No one realized at the time that sick people needed their blood to help them recover from their illnesses, and that the leeches were in fact far more harmful than helpful. David, who had been a strong man, weakened under the strain of daily bleedings.

The doctor was impressed with Clara's serious and mature attitude in the sickroom. He permitted her not only to give various medicines to David, but also to apply the leeches herself, an astonishing responsibility for an eleven-year-old. Clara never flinched during these daily operations, and the Bartons marveled at her quiet courage. This, after all, was the same girl who had grown up terrified of snakes and thunderstorms. Suddenly, in her service to someone else, she had stopped thinking of herself completely.

During the two years of David's recovery, Clara spent almost all her time in the sickroom with him. Occasionally she broke away long enough to go for a gallop on her favorite pony, but otherwise she remained a watchful and attentive nurse. She loved the feeling of serving someone else. It made her feel useful and deserving in a way nothing else ever had.

When Clara was thirteen, the doctors decided to dis-

16

continue the treatment with the leeches and administer a new kind of water therapy. Without the daily drain on his blood, David began, finally, to recover. When the doctors decided that he was out of danger, Clara was released from her nursing duties.

She was by now grown to her full adult height — five feet tall. Others of her age had grown much taller in the Massachusetts sunshine, but Clara had spent two years almost exclusively indoors, and some people believed that that time might have inhibited her growth. She was pale and tiny — but her nursing experience had excited her more than anything else she'd ever done. Now that she could once more enjoy her freedom, she was bored.

The Bartons did not realize how devoted Clara had become to her service, until a hired man in the village fell sick with smallpox. Before they could object to her interference, Clara had gone to work as his nurse. Suddenly her eyes were alive and sparkling again, and her skin glowing with excitement. In the course of her nursing duties, she caught smallpox, but it was a mild case. She hurried back to work as soon as the doctors released her from bed.

A pattern had begun, one which would continue throughout her life. Clara found her greatest satisfaction in serving others, in throwing herself into the needs of the moment and finding practical, common-sense answers to the most pressing problems. She loved the feeling of being able to help someone who was weak, ill or tired, of knowing that her hands were strong enough and firm enough to provide whatever was necessary. She loved facing a dilemma and deciding how to handle it.

From the age of eleven on, Clara Barton was at her best when serving others. Serving without any thought for herself would soon become the foundation of her life.

3

A Different Kind of Teacher

THROUGHOUT HER LATE teens, while she was nursing friends and neighbors, Clara found herself happy and comfortable. However, in periods of idleness, she reverted to her old shyness, which still remained painful.

Clara had by now returned to school in North Oxford. She continued to live at home on the Learned farm with only her parents for company. Mrs. Learned and her children had moved away. Stephen and David now owned a mill in the nearby town of Oxford. Stephen was married, and he, his wife, and David still lived at the original Barton farm. Sally was also married, and she now lived with her husband on the other side of North Oxford. Dolly, who had been gradually wasting away from a severe depression for five years, had eventually died in 1842.

All this affected young Clara deeply. While her grades in school remained excellent, she felt awkward and uncomfortable in social situations. She began keeping a diary, into which she poured her most confidential feelings. Often the diary entries recorded her feelings of sadness and depression, of feeling unneeded and unwanted by anyone. These were the same feelings that Clara's sister Dolly used to suffer from. It was obvious, even to her family, that something needed to be done.

At the time, there was a new science developing in the Western world, called phrenology. Phrenology was the study of the shape of the human skull, which some people believed would reveal secrets of character and personality. There was really no reason for this belief, since the brain, rather than the shape of the skull, determines these things. However, phrenologists were stubborn in their beliefs and persuasive in their explanations.

One of the foremost phrenologists of the time was Lorenzo N. Fowler, an Englishman who came to lecture throughout the United States about the new science. Mrs. Barton invited him to stay at their home for part of the tour. Coincidentally Clara was staying at home most of the time, too — recovering from a case of the mumps.

She overheard her mother conversing with Mr. Fowler and expressing her anxiety about her youngest daughter and her shyness. Mr. Fowler had had an opportunity to observe Clara closely during his visit. When Mrs. Barton asked for his opinion about Clara, he was ready to speak out.

Clara was lying on a couch in the next room, and she never forgot Mr. Fowler's words. He told Mrs. Barton that Clara would be sensitive all her life, and that she would never fight for herself. However, he added, where others were concerned she would always fight battles fearlessly. He suggested that the family give Clara more responsibility. She had all the makings of a teacher. Why not find her a school where she could teach?

Clara quaked at the thought of facing a roomful of children, but her parents were impressed with Fowler's suggestion. They began to look into possibilities and found that a one-room school near Sally's home would soon be needing a teacher.

Clara finished her own schooling within a year and applied for a certificate to teach at the school. At that time, teachers were not required to attend college or take formal, written examinations. All that a teacher needed to qualify for a teaching position was to pass an examination in front of a clergyman, lawyer, and justice of the peace in town.

So Clara appeared in front of the three fearsome men of District Number 9 to take their examination. She was only seventeen, and she was concerned that her lack of height would make her look too young for the job. Her mother, sisters, and women friends helped by lengthening her skirts and piling her hair on her head to give her a more dignified stature. She passed the examination easily and began to prepare herself for the ordeal of facing forty strange youngsters when school opened.

Clara was particularly concerned with the gossip she had heard about four older boys who attended the school. According to her friends, these boys had made life miserable for the school's previous teacher, and had eventually even locked her out and taken over themselves. Clara was warned that they were bullies and that she should be on her guard.

Naturally, this did not help to calm her fears. If anything, Clara was more worried than ever. Her parents had agreed that it would be smart for her to live with Sally, whose home was close to the schoolhouse, and she found herself being uprooted for the first time since she moved to the Learned farm. Now she lived in a new home, away from her parents for the first time, and faced a new job. How could she do it?

On the morning of her first day, Clara put on a brand-new dress of bright green, which her mother and friends had made for her. It was long and full, giving her the appropriate look of maturity, but nothing she wore could calm the rapid beating of her heart as she approached the schoolhouse. There was no one in the schoolyard, but she could hear giggles and whispers from inside the tiny wooden building. Steeling herself, Clara opened the door — and stopped dead on the threshold.

Forty children of various ages stared back at her from their desks. Some looked curious or interested; some snickered. In the back, the four boys Clara had heard about smirked at her. They were already anticipating an easy victory over this tiny — and obviously terrified — new teacher.

Clara had written and rehearsed a little welcoming speech to deliver to her new students, but in those first awful moments, every word of it fled from her mind. Unable to think clearly, she stumbled forward to the teacher's desk at the front. Her eye caught sight of the Bible, and she opened it, thankful that it was there. She knew she could not speak to her class without stammering, but she could read to them.

She read to the class, and suddenly, in the stillness, her confidence came back. She glanced at the four boys in back. They looked away. It was going to be all right, she thought. When she had finished the chapter, she plunged straight into her prepared lessons. The children did as she told them.

During the noontime recess many of the students remained in the schoolyard to play games, including the four boys. They had started their own game of ball. Clara asked to join them. David's lessons in sports were still vivid in her mind.

In a few minutes, the four boys were turning astonished eyes on one another. Their new teacher could pitch a ball better than they could, and run faster. In fact, she could do everything better than they could. She said later that "when they found that if they won a game it was because I permitted it, their respect knew no bounds."

There was no question, after that, of any problem with the boys. They liked Clara so much that they became model students. They carried her books home in the afternoons, ran errands for her, and did their lessons as faithfully and carefully as the tiniest tot in the schoolroom.

At the end of the school term, Clara was praised for her work in District Number 9. Her school was the best-disciplined and best-run in the community.

Clara was astonished. "There hasn't been any discipline!" she declared. "I haven't disciplined anyone!"

Perhaps not. The town authorities, however, began to regard Clara as an excellent person to work with troubled classes, and now they requested that she work through a summer session in Charlton, a nearby village. The Charlton children were noisy and wild, and the school board hoped Clara could calm them down.

Teaching in Charlton meant that Clara would have to move again in order to live within a comfortable distance of her new assignment. It would be the first time she was living without any member of her family nearby. She boarded at a home in Charlton, where the people were cheerful and comforting, which helped her feel a little better about the separation.

The school, however, was another case of students testing their teacher for weaknesses. From the first day Clara saw the hints of rebellion in the fifty students, especially among several of the older boys. She gritted her teeth and tried to continue her planned lessons, but the bigger boys would not let her alone. When Clara smiled at them and treated them as she had her North Oxford students, they jeered at her.

Clara could not make a success of her Charlton class unless she tamed the boys who were disrupting it. She decided to focus on the ringleader, a tall, swarthy boy who urged his friends on to pranks. Clara tried to reach his mother, to ask for her help in disciplining the boy. Her attempt was useless.

So Clara steeled her nerves and took matters into her own hands. She had never even considered hitting one of her students, though that was standard practice in the schoolroom of those days. Clara had always felt that mutual respect between teacher and student worked far better than intimidation. Now, though, she had no choice.

When the ringleader strolled into the classroom late

the next morning, Clara asked him to step forward to her desk. He laughed boldly as he came down the aisle — but his laughter choked off when Clara withdrew a riding whip from her desk.

Clara had never before needed or wanted to use any form of physical punishment, and she hated to use it now, but for several minutes Clara wielded the whip, humbling the school bully. The bully finally apologized to the class for his interruptions, but the violence was too much for Clara. She dismissed the class for the day and took them for a picnic outdoors.

She never forgot that whipping. Seventy years later, she remembered that "all these years have not been able to efface [it]. I had learnt what discipline meant, and it was for all time so far as that school was concerned; none ever needed more than a kindly smile." As was typical of her, Clara had seen the need to perform an unpleasant task and had risen to the occasion herself. It would not be the last time that she turned her hand to a task others would not do.

For the next ten years Clara kept busy teaching in various schools around Oxford. She was the teacher requested for the most difficult schools, and she was always successful in directing her students' interest from mischief to serious study. Yet there was a restless streak in her. Once a school began to run smoothly, Clara was not interested in maintaining it. She always wanted to push on to a new challenge.

Naturally, Clara had other interests besides her teaching. She kept up her childhood enthusiasm for horses and rode every day on the saddle horse her father kept for her. A less active pastime was picking blackberries and chestnuts. The roads around Oxford were filled with blackberries and, in autumn, with chestnuts. Strolling along with baskets in the company of a friend and collecting the natural treats was one of Clara's best-loved pursuits. She was a poor card player, and unlike many ladies of the time, not very clever at painting, or making artificial flowers by hand. Clara preferred exercising her intelligence.

She loved to write letters, and throughout her life kept up lengthy correspondences with members of her family, friends, and acquaintances she met in the course of her work. In later years she would send out pages of observations written from the battlefields, hospitals, and disaster sites she visited. Now, however, in young womanhood, her letters were filled with chatty comments on her teaching, local friends, and her family.

Along with letter writing, Clara also showed a flair for verse. She enjoyed composing rhymes, though she made no claims for their quality. She simply found great pleasure in jotting down these verses. It was a habit she continued all her life.

Though she was often busier than other women around Oxford, Clara did not lack for male friends. She enjoyed the company of men who found her witty and charming. Though her figure was small and square, and her only real physical asset was a mane of thick, dark hair, a few men courted her persistently.

Clara enjoyed their attention and attended picnics, dinners, and parties with them. However, unlike many women of the time who depended on men to take care of them, she did not feel the need to marry simply for financial security. Clara had been earning her own living since she was seventeen. She knew she could continue to take care of herself for as long as was necessary.

In addition, men of that time expected women to agree with them in all matters. Women were thought to be inferior to men in intelligence and emotional stability. Men particularly pursued women who allowed them to believe they were helpless and in need of male guidance and protection.

Clara, however, was a woman raised by men to be their equal. She had been educated in a family where she was taught always to do her best. In fact, she was severely criticized if she did not. She was a very intelligent woman and could not hide her own lively curiosity in order to please a man. Therefore, there were very few men she could consider possible husbands.

A few men found themselves seriously infatuated with Clara. Her dark, lovely hair and sympathetic demeanor caught their attention. A number of these suitors asked her to marry them. She always refused. In the course of her life, she met and befriended many special men, but the one man who was her perfect complement did not appear. Marriage and children were a separate career that Clara was unable to achieve.

However, she continually sought new opportunities. Her next challenge came through her family. By now her two brothers, Stephen and David, were successful in business. The mill they owned was doing very well, and they employed many workers, including youngsters. This was common practice at the time. Unfortunately, the mill children seldom attended any kind of school at all. They were so busy working side by side with their parents that there was never any time to study.

Clara saw the problems of these children. She was concerned that they had no way of learning. She became convinced that if they were not given the chance to study and better themselves, they couldn't use their talents constructively, and would eventually become dangerous to the community.

As Mr. Fowler had predicted years before, Clara was a fighter on behalf of other people. She wanted to set up a school for the mill children, and she went to her brother Stephen for permission. Though he agreed with her about the necessity of educating these youngsters, many others in the Oxford community did not. Many of the elders — including Clara's father — believed that it was a waste of time and money to try to educate the lower social classes. They did not want to spend precious dollars from the school budget for such a project.

Clara and Stephen Jr. fought the school board for a year. They argued in favor of the mill children with anyone who would listen. Finally, on a momentous night, the issue came before the board for a vote. Captain Barton was moderating the discussion, and though he had clearly spoken in opposition to his children's desire, some community members wondered whether he would be swayed by the fact that Clara and Stephen were his children.

Captain Barton was not. However, he and many others had underestimated Clara's persistence and drive to get what she wanted. She had persuaded factory workers to turn out in time to vote on the issue. Eighty-two of them marched into the meeting room just in time to deposit the votes that swung the issue in Clara's favor. She got a school for her mill children.

One of the large local mills reluctantly gave her a small room in a corner of their factory as a schoolroom. Clara organized classes and ended up teaching seventy students of several nationalities and ages. She taught them not only reading, writing, and arithmetic, but also skills such as bookkeeping and subjects like philosophy, chemistry, and history.

Eventually, once she had again proved her mettle in a worthy battle, Clara became restless. Her qualifications as a teacher were strictly limited. She knew that she was not as educated as she would like to be. She reasoned that she would become a better teacher if she knew more herself. She felt it was time to remedy that problem with some more studying.

It was also time to leave home. Clara was tired of being called on to step into a new school when there was a problem. She needed to expand her own horizons and see more of the world than the community around Oxford, Massachusetts. She was twenty-nine years old. It was time to set off on her own.

The Clinton Liberal Institute in Clinton, New York offered a course of study that appealed to Clara. It was also two hundred miles from home, which meant that she would not be back except for the most important reasons. In December, Clara packed her trunk and huddled under a warm quilt in the family sleigh. Stephen, sitting next to her, drove her to the Worcester railroad depot.

As Clara stepped onto the bottom rung of the train, clutching her satchel, neither she nor the waving Stephen realized just how far she would be going.

4

The World Grows Wider

THE FIRST WEEKS away from home were anxious and lonely ones for Clara. She had expected to begin classes at Clinton on the first Monday in January, but Clinton was rebuilding its facilities for female students. This delayed the opening of the term for several weeks.

During these weeks, Clara settled into a tiny temporary room in Clinton House, a boarding house that rented rooms to Clinton students, and passed the time alone. Once more her shyness returned. She spent many lonely nights in her little room, writing carefully cheerful letters home to her family to assure them that she was doing well. Often, as she wrote, she wondered what they would say if they knew the truth.

Finally, the Clinton renovation was complete and the interrupted school term was about to begin. There was a brand-new building, the White Seminary, composed of dormitory rooms as well as classrooms for female students. Clara, relieved, moved into one of the dormitory rooms and began to feel more cheerful about her new life.

Clinton students paid thirty-five dollars per semester. This price included tuition, room, board, and laundry fees. While male and female students were not permitted to attend the same lectures, women were allowed to study most of the same subjects the men did, which pleased Clara greatly. Subjects included analytic geometry, languages, philosophy, astronomy, and ancient history.

Clara's intense desire to learn conflicted with the Institute's policy of limiting the number of subjects a female student could undertake at one time. However, Clara pleaded to add extra courses to her schedule. She was so persuasive that Clinton's principal, Louise Barker, finally gave in to her request. Clara happily settled down to a heavy course load. As in her earlier school days, she proved to be an excellent student.

Clara was so busy studying and working that she might have easily missed any social activities at Clinton whatsoever. Louise Barker took a personal interest in her, though. She insisted that Clara leave her books occasionally in order to refresh herself among the other students.

Since many of them were both younger than Clara and also worldlier, she often felt shy around them and sometimes shrank from meeting them, even though many were quite friendly to her. Curiously, she was reluctant to mention her teaching experience to any of her fellow students. She keenly felt the age difference between herself and her fellow students, and believed that any remark about her past would further separate her from them. She also did not want to alarm her teachers by revealing that she had been a teacher, too. To the laughing, joking youngsters who sat beside her in classes, she was a rather odd older woman who ate only two meals a day in order to maintain her figure, and wore vivid green dresses to class.

Clara's time at Clinton might have remained very lonely, if not for a few cherished friendships that she formed there. An intense friendship developed between her and a young Quaker student, Mary Norton, of Hightstown, New Jersey. She also enjoyed many lighthearted moments with Abby Barker of Connecticut. These two women were her friends and would remain supporters for the rest of her life.

Clara also attracted a fair amount of attention from the Clinton men. She rode horseback with Samuel Ramsey, a mathematics professor at nearby Hamilton College and attended parties with Charles Norton, Mary's brother and a Clinton student as well. While Clara enjoyed spending social hours with them, she did not regard either as a serious suitor. They both became attached to her, but she gently discouraged any relationship beyond friendship. She was too absorbed in her studies for romantic interests.

All that was abruptly shattered in May, 1851. On opening a letter from home, she discovered that her oldest brother Stephen had been indicted on charges of bank robbery in upstate New York. For some time Oxford townspeople had gossiped about the amount of real estate holdings Stephen and David had managed to acquire. Such holdings were expensive, and the prof-

33

its from the Barton's business did not seem to be large enough to support them.

Stephen, who had proudly held a position as town leader in Oxford, was now in disgrace. In addition, his creditors were calling in their debts, fearful that he might go to prison. Should that happen, the creditors would lose any money that was owed to them.

Stephen did not go to prison. He was cleared of the robbery charge. However, in those days, once someone was accused of a crime, doubts always lingered in people's minds regardless of whether or not the accused was found guilty. Just being accused was shame enough, and his disgrace affected Clara deeply. In later years, people thought her to be shy about her accomplishments. Actually, she was not, but to draw attention to herself might also draw attention to her brother. She dreaded any mention of his disgrace. Therefore, she shielded him as best she could by deflecting questions about herself that might have led to questions about her family. Her reputation for modesty and humility date from this incident and her terror that someone might disclose mention of it.

Clara had not yet recovered from the shock of her brother's disgrace when she received word in July that her mother Sarah had passed away. Clara had known that her mother was ill, but she did not realize how swiftly the illness was taking its toll. Coming on top of the news of Stephen's problems, this new sorrow sapped the last of Clara's strength. She locked herself in her room for a week and spoke to no one.

As a result of these two family problems, Clara decided to leave Clinton. She had learned a great deal and delighted in her studies, but now her savings were dwindling. She believed her family was in disarray and needed her support. She decided it was time to go home.

It was a rude awakening for Clara to arrive in North Oxford at the end of the summer of 1851. The family she had believed was grief stricken had made adjustments without her. Her father now lived with her brother David and his wife. Her sister Sally was absorbed in raising two sons. Her family was managing perfectly well without her help.

Clara's sensitive nature felt rebuffed by the self-sufficiency she saw all around her. She interpreted her relatives' independence as coldness toward her. She felt there was no place for her anymore in North Oxford. No one seemed to need her except the small, one-room schoolhouses — and after her term at Clinton she didn't want to go back to those. Reluctantly, she packed her trunk once more.

Mary Norton, Clara's close chum at Clinton, eagerly invited her to spend part of her vacation with her family in Hightstown, New Jersey. Clara accepted and found herself for the first time in the midst of a warm, openly affectionate family circle. Unlike her own family, which was bound by work, the Norton family was bound by love. Clara thrived on their kindness and interest.

Despite her pleasure in the Norton household, however, Clara knew she would soon have to seek a new job. In October, 1851, still living with the Nortons, she took up teaching once again at the Cedarville School, located near the Norton farm. It was her most successful teaching effort to date.

Clara told her students from the beginning that she

expected them to behave well. To underscore this, she asked the biggest and toughest boy in school to help her break all of the rods and switches that previous teachers used to discipline unruly students. When the switches lay broken outside, Clara set about organizing classes with her usual competence. The students, many of whom were teenagers, immediately leaped in to help. She had proven to them her confidence in their good behavior. They responded with a wild eagerness to study.

It disturbed Clara that her services at Cedarville were paid for by the students themselves. Unlike Massachusetts, New Jersey had not established a free-school system. Those who could not pay did not attend school.

Also, her life at the Norton farm was becoming difficult for her. Warm and kind though they were, Clara found it impossible to spend every moment in the company of the Norton family. While they cheerfully wrote letters, played games and musical instruments and did household chores together, she often felt the need for privacy. The Nortons, comfortable in their socializing, did not really understand this attitude.

When the Cedarville school term ended on April 20, 1852, Clara packed her trunk yet again. The Nortons bid her a cheerful farewell, expecting her to return after a few short weeks' visit elsewhere. Clara knew, however, that she would not return. She was grateful for their kindness to her, but it was time to move on.

In late May, Clara arrived in Bordentown, New Jersey, only ten miles from Hightstown. She had chosen the town for no particular reason. As she walked the streets, she saw knots of boys lounging against buildings and apparently at loose ends. When she asked why they were not in school, they answered, "Lady, there is no school for us." It was time, she decided, to start a model school demonstrating the superiority of a free-school system like the one in Massachusetts.

Marshaling every argument she could, Clara presented herself to members of the school board and won them over to the idea of a free school in Bordentown. She was back on familiar ground, fighting a battle on behalf of someone else. As usual with such battles, Clara won. The school board did not have to pay her a salary or donate materials. They would simply provide a building in which she could hold classes. She would do the rest. Skeptical but impressed with her poise and determination, the school board found her a dilapidated brick schoolhouse on Crosswicks Street and waited to see what she would do.

In early July, 1852, Clara announced the opening of her new school. On her first morning, there were only six very reluctant boys waiting for her in the school-yard. Clara invited them into the classroom like a Pied Piper. She talked soothingly of the world's mountains and oceans, pointed out countries on a big colorful map, and told dramatic stories to get the boys to stay. She said nothing about books, or studying, or homework.

The strategy worked. The next morning there were twenty boys waiting for her in the schoolyard. By the end of the week there were forty. At the end of the second week there were fifty-five. Young girls were begging to be allowed to attend classes as well. Clara pushed aside desks and shoved chairs together to make room.

She even gave up her own chair to an eager young student. The experiment was working brilliantly.

A year later Clara was supervising the building of a brand-new public schoolhouse in Bordentown. The new school would house six hundred students. She had proved without a doubt that youngsters given an opportunity to learn will do so. Now she was reaping the benefits of her demonstration.

It was a blow to learn that she was not to be the school's first principal. Clara had operated for years in a society where women were considered second-class citizens. Yet she herself had accomplished a remarkable amount simply on the strength of her own will and intelligence. Few women could have achieved what she achieved, because society limited women's roles so greatly.

Now it was a shock for Clara to realize that the school board was bowing to social pressure in appointing a man, J. Kirby Burnham, as principal. Clara was to work as his "female assistant." She was hurt and bewildered that the school board would place anyone above her, especially since it was she who had fought for the school to begin with.

Yet Mr. Fowler's long-ago prediction about her was again proving correct. Clara could not fight battles on her own behalf, no matter how strongly and persistently she fought for others. She disliked Burnham, whose discipline was harsh and inflexible. She resented the disparity between his salary and hers: He was being paid more than twice what she received. Finally, she did not believe that he was either fair or impartial enough to run the school correctly.

Burnham, knowing Clara's influence, resented her as well. He undercut her at every opportunity and threw his support to others who had arguments with her. Soon, the atmosphere between them became unbearably strained.

The result was that Clara completely lost her voice. When she tried to speak, nothing but a whispered croak emerged from her lips. Despite all the remedies she tried, she could not speak.

No teacher can teach effectively without a voice. There was nothing for Clara to do but resign from the school and try to regain her strength. It was a relief to leave behind the rivalries and jealousies of Bordentown, but she regretted not being able to finish what she had started.

Right now the most important consideration was her health. Clara wanted to be able to speak again and to recover the strength she had lost in her bitter battles in Bordentown. Once more she set off with little more than a hazy idea of her destination.

She expected, once recovered, to be able to return to teaching again. But once Clara stepped into the muddy streets of Washington, D.C., she turned her back forever on the teaching profession. Now she would be serving others in an entirely different way.

5

A Woman in a Man's World

IN 1854, WASHINGTON, D.C. was changing from the small peaceful village it once was into a troubled city. As the country grew larger and more diversified, Washington became the center of a series of raging controversies between North and South.

When thirty-two-year-old Clara Barton entered the Capital city, she was overwhelmed by the turmoil. Unlike the villages and little towns she had lived in previously, Washington seemed to be a mass of people all busy with their own problems. Clara was fascinated by the variety of people around her. The rush of activity stimulated her, and the warm climate of the city soothed her tired body.

Her voice was still weak, though, which meant she could not yet freely socialize among the government men and their wives. However, she did not need her voice in order to listen to others. And listen she did, spending many days as a visitor in the gallery high above the main floor of Congress. The burning issue of the day was slavery.

Here Clara heard the passionate arguments of Southern representatives, who favored expanding the slavery system that supported the Southern plantations and farms. New territories were applying for statehood, and Congress had to decide whether or not these territories would be slave states or free states. The Southerners, naturally, wanted the new states to be slave states.

Clara also heard the fiery speeches of Northern representatives. Over the years, the North had become far more industrial than the agricultural South. Northerners needed no slave labor to support their economy. They saw the institution of slavery as sinful. Many were committed to the abolition of slavery — or at least, to limiting it to the Southern states. Northern representatives were outraged at the Southern desire to expand slavery into new territories applying for statehood.

Clara was a little confused by all the controversy. However, her quick mind noted many of the tricks of the speakers on the floor. She stored away vivid memories of Congressmen drawling lazy arguments and shouting declarations at the top of their lungs. She combed through newspapers for the statements of other influential men. In all her reading and listening, she was learning valuable lessons about the presentation of issues. In short, she was learning to persuade. It was a quality she would prize in years to come, when she fought so many battles among government men with nothing to recommend her but an excellent grasp of the facts and an eloquent manner.

Meanwhile, as she listened to the various Congressmen, Clara began to enjoy a new sense of well-being. Now that she was removed from the pressures that had worn her down, her energy and interest in the world returned. She could speak again without effort. She ate hearty meals and slept long dreamless hours.

As usual, however, when Clara felt herself well enough, she began to feel restless. She wasn't comfortable spending her time just listening to others when she knew she was once more capable of working. It was time to find a job.

Schoolteaching, her first idea, was more difficult work to secure in Washington. Schools were already well established and functioning without the help of a teacher who was accustomed to walking into chaos and creating order. There seemed to be no place for Clara in the Washington school system. Yet she liked the city. She determined that she would remain there, and decided to find another kind of work.

Washington was then, as it is today, a very political place. Most of the employment available stemmed directly from government, and government jobs were often given more on the basis of political influence than on the strength of the applicant's ability.

Clara quickly realized that she would need a champion in order to win one of these jobs. She turned for help to a friend of her father's, Alexander DeWitt, a Congressman from Massachusetts. DeWitt introduced her to Charles Mason, who was the commissioner of patents. Before long, Clara persuaded him to hire her as a temporary clerk in the Patent Office, where new inventions are registered with the government.

For the first time since the beginning of her professional life, Clara was situated among men in a competitive atmosphere. In her teaching days she had actually commanded the same salary as a male teacher doing the same job. However, she had never faced a male teacher in the same classroom at his own level. In the Patent Office, she competed with men every day. She was as competent as they were, and she earned the same salary they did. Furthermore, she was one of the few women in any kind of government service. Other women who worked in branches of the government were widows or daughters of workers who had died. They continued the job in his name. Unlike them, Clara was an independent woman securing a job in her own name. It was bound to cause trouble among the other workers.

Yet the first few months fascinated her. She wrote to a friend in October, 1854, "My situation is delightfully pleasant. There is nothing in the world connected with it to trouble me and not a single disagreeable thing to do, and no one to complain of me." She worked from nine in the morning to three in the afternoon. For much of that time, Clara, in company with the other clerks, bent over ledgers with long quill pens, copying information at the rate of ten cents per hundred words. The work required an exacting eye and clear, legible handwriting. Clara had both. As a result, she was one of the highest-paid clerks in the office.

Then, in mid-July of 1855, after she had been employed for about a year, Commissioner Mason resigned his position and left Washington to return to his home in Iowa. Suddenly Clara had no champion in the Patent Office. The acting commissioner, although a friend of hers, was anxious to please his superior, Secretary of the Interior Robert McClelland, who oversaw the functions of the Patent Office. McClelland hated the idea of women working in offices. Therefore, the acting commissioner set about removing those women from their jobs.

Clara found herself working as a copyist at home, instead of in the office. Her pay was reduced, but McClelland was satisfied as long as she was away from the office. Fortunately, Charles Mason returned from Iowa in November, and Clara soon found herself back in the office on a full-time basis.

By now Clara was the only woman left in the Patent Office. Her capacity for hard work had not endeared her to the other, male clerks around her. To make matters worse, Mason asked her to help him weed out the dishonest and less industrious workers in the office. As lazy male clerks began to lose their jobs, they blamed Clara.

Suddenly the Patent Office was no longer a pleasant place to work. Clara found herself the target of nasty lies. Gossips around the office whispered tales about her and her close ties with Mason. The men lining the hallway of the office blew smoke in her face, spat tobacco juice at her skirts and muttered insults as she passed.

Clara, always the crusader for other people, once again would not raise a hand in her own behalf. She could only ignore the insults and the crude stories circulating about her. She was determined to persevere in the job, if only to prove that she would not be driven out of it by malicious gossip. Fortunately, Charles Mason believed firmly in her abilities and her character. Her efficiency and honesty were unquestionable.

Yet it became an effort for Clara to drag herself to her desk. The backstabbing and undermining of the others was wearing her down.

The work load, also, was becoming a strain. Clerks in the Patent Office were overworked with copying. Clara, one of the best and fastest, found herself copying over a thousand pages a month, straining her eyes and raising large ugly calluses on her fingers. Even when she came down with malaria, a possibly deadly disease, she continued to work through the fevers, frequently making up time by copying late into the night.

In 1856 James Buchanan was elected president. He took office in March of 1857. By this time new political appointments were rumored throughout the branches of government. Clara's job was once more in jeopardy. To make matters more perilous, both Charles Mason and Alexander DeWitt resigned their positions and left Washington.

Clara saw that it would be impossible for her to hold on for much longer. As a woman, she would automatically be dismissed by the next person in the patent commissioner's job. As a personal target of animosity, she could not hope for any further intervention on her behalf.

In September 1857 she was formally dismissed by the Patent Office. With little regret, Clara set off for a short visit with her family.

She had intended to spend only a few weeks in North Oxford. Yet her visit extended for over two years. She found her family sadly changed. Her father was growing deaf and blind. Her brother Stephen, having been cleared of the robbery charges, had gone in 1856 to live

46

in North Carolina and start a milling complex there to escape the shame. Clara missed him a great deal. She also felt once more the cold, lonely sensation of being an outsider among busy and productive people. Each member of her family was going ahead with his or her own life.

Clara, idle once more, began to sink into depression. There seemed to be no place for her in North Oxford. She had no job, no occupation of any kind, no interest to keep her busy. She turned to classes in French and drawing for some distraction, but neither brought her much relief from her unhappiness.

As always with Clara's health, her depression led to physical weakness, which left her debilitated for several months. By the time she felt sufficiently recovered, the elections of November 1860 had come and gone. A Republican lawyer named Abraham Lincoln would become the next president, in March of 1861. Once more the politics of the moment swayed the decisions of Washington's officeholders. Clara was summoned back to her old position at the Patent Office.

Clara had no idea that at the age of thirty-nine, she was on the verge of beginning her real career.

6

Nursing the Wounded

FOR MANY YEARS, the North and South had grown steadily different from each other in their politics and economies. As a result, battles raged over the twin issues of slavery and states' rights. The South wanted a system that gave more power to the individual states instead of the central federal government. They also wanted to keep slavery. Now, with the election of an unpopular Republican president, opposed to both of the South's demands, Clara watched with dismay as bitter words turned to bloodshed.

Abraham Lincoln took the oath of office in March, 1861. With Lincoln in office, the South knew they had little hope of peacefully getting what they wanted. A month later, Southern forces fired on Northern soldiers at Fort Sumter in Charleston, South Carolina. A number of Southern states officially declared that they were no longer part of the United States. The North announced they would fight to take those states back. The American Civil War had begun.

It was some time, however, before a major battle took place. Both the Union in the North, and the Confederacy to the South, needed time to raise, equip and drill armies. Washington, which was not only the nation's capital but also located uncomfortably close to the rebelling states, became an even more exciting — and dangerous — city to live in.

Clara had hoped that reason would prevail and that the Southern states would agree, somehow, to remain a part of the Union. However, when the rebel forces fired on Fort Sumter, all reason appeared to vanish overnight. Both sides poured frantic effort into providing their fighting men with weapons and supplies.

However, provisions were neither as plentiful nor as convenient as the armies needed. The Confederacy boasted excellent crops with which to feed its soldiers, but it was pitifully inadequate in producing cannon or ammunition, since there were almost no iron foundries in the South.

The North, on the other hand, had many industries to turn out war supplies. They believed their army was far better equipped to handle the ravages of battle, with every modern device to feed, clothe, and shelter their soldiers. The War Department boasted that their medical supplies and doctors were more than adequate to deal with battlefield emergencies.

Clara saw firsthand exactly how the "well-stocked" army was equipped. On April 19, a week after the firing at Fort Sumter, troops from the Sixth Massachusetts Regiment arrived in Baltimore.

Baltimore supported the Southern feelings about seceding, or separating, from the Union and forming their own country. Rebels from the city jeered at the train-load of Union soldiers, openly pelting them with bricks and rocks and shouting insults.

The Union officers ordered their men to refrain from firing unless first fired upon. The rebels, however, did more than enough damage without aiming a rifle. Three Union soldiers were killed by the mob and thirty others were wounded. Not only were these the war's first casualties, but the rebels also managed to destroy the army's luggage, which contained the only light clothing the troops had.

The Sixth Massachusetts Regiment hastily retreated to Washington, where the news of the attack had preceded them by telegraph. Clara was horrified by what she heard. Some of the soldiers were boys she remembered from her North Oxford teaching days. She decided she had to give whatever aid she could.

In Washington, citizens and government workers hurried frantically to provide temporary shelters for the frightened, bleeding, raw recruits who had so proudly ridden the rails to Baltimore that day. There were no provisions for the soldiers, and conditions were makeshift, at best. Clara and her sister Sally, who was visiting, hurried to the depot of the Baltimore and Ohio Railroad, where the train brought in the tired and frightened men. The floor of the Capitol Building had been hastily fitted up to house them.

It was the first time Clara would ever look on a sight of confusion, fear and helpless wounded men. It was perhaps the mildest example of that condition that she would see throughout the war, but it was shocking enough.

For what would be the first of many times, Clara surveyed the rows of military men, trying to decide what they needed most. Men with familiar faces called out to her and she greeted them with the same warmth and friendliness they remembered from her teaching days. What did they need — what could she do for them?

The soldiers told her that with their luggage stolen, they had nothing to wear but heavy woolen undergarments. It was already springtime in Washington. The warm air, combined with the soldiers' thick clothes, was causing severe discomfort. In addition, they'd been issued no rations at all, not even a cup of water. They were dirty, hot and hungry. Clara listened carefully. Then she disappeared.

When Clara returned, she brought with her a number of servants, carrying boxes of cotton underwear, along with combs, sewing utensils, needle and thread, candles, and other useful items. She had risen early to shop at neighboring groceries for food. At the sight of her provisions, the grateful men broke into a cheer.

Clara distributed her supplies at once. When the men had been made more comfortable and satisfied their hunger, she climbed into the chair reserved for the president of the Senate. She had brought with her a copy of the *Worcester Spy*, a daily Massachusetts newspaper. With thousands of eyes on her, the once-timid woman read the paper aloud in a strong, clear voice.

It was a momentous turn in Clara's life. From childhood, Captain Barton had taught her that "next to Heaven our highest duty was . . . to serve our country and . . . support its laws." Now her patriotic fervor combined with her own deep-seated need to serve others.

The need for her services — and the services of others like her — was enormous. When the war began, there was not a single trained nurse in the United States. Busy surgeons, working long hours, assisted each other in ministering to patients. When they were too absorbed in their surgery, the patients were left unattended. Days might pass before wounded men were fed, bathed or given a cup of water.

Yet the government stubbornly believed that the system they had set up was the only workable one. When their armies went on the march, the medical supply wagon was often the last in the train. It might take days for the bandages, ointments and medicines to reach the men who fell on the battlefield.

Hospitals provisioned for the wounded were located too far away to be able to offer immediate relief. Army surgeons working directly at the battle sites were the only help offered the wounded. They set up makeshift tents wherever they could find room away from the roar of the cannon. Conditions were filthy. Often, there were only a few doctors per thousand wounded men. It was impossible to save as many men as they could have with more help and better supplies.

In the first months of the war, however, Clara did not think about the battlefield. She loved the military atmosphere around Washington, where many troops were quartered while they drilled and prepared for battle. At this time her older sister Sally was living temporarily with her in Washington. She and Sally spent long days visiting the troops, reading to them, joking with them, in an effort to keep up their spirits.

The soldiers' main complaint was the lack of food.

Clara's presence had become so familiar during her visits that wives and mothers of the soldiers began to send her their care packages. They trusted Clara to deliver their parcels, rather than sending them to the army quartermaster, whose work was slipshod at best. Soon Clara found herself in the middle of a clearinghouse of supplies, all of which she faithfully delivered as swiftly as she received them.

The next step was obvious. Clara notified the local Massachusetts newspapers that she would be glad to receive supplies for the soldiers, which she would take responsibility to distribute. Almost overnight, items of all description began to pour into her quarters in Washington. Soon Clara found herself so hemmed in by cartons and boxes that she could hardly move around her own room. She rented a larger room to hold the overflow. At the same time, she found the business of distributing the parcels to be time-consuming work. As a result, with little regret, she decided to take a leave of absence from her job at the Patent Office.

Clara spent her days in hospital wards around Washington, passing out her supplies and cheering the patients with every comfort she could think of. She found herself enjoying the contact with the men and reveling in their gratitude. Without realizing it, she was beginning to move toward direct service on the battlefield.

This was prompted partly by the actions of one of Clara's friends and former landladies, Almira Fales. Mrs. Fales, an early collector of supplies for the soldiers, determined that the hospitals far from the front were liberally stocked. Men on the battlefield, however, closer to the line of fire, needed all the parcels and nursing she could give them. Mrs. Fales began to make forays close to the front, to tend those who needed help immediately.

Clara followed her example, realizing, like Mrs. Fales, the desperate need for nurses close to the action. All her feelings of patriotism, loyalty, and love of service rose to form one stubborn resolution. She applied to the government for passes to the front.

At the time, the Union government was busy reassuring itself that it was, in fact, providing every possible necessity to its armies. Government officials told each other that no army in the world was better stocked or attended than theirs. Clara's request, therefore, was a slap in the face to those beliefs. She was telling them in no uncertain terms that the army needed more help than the government was providing.

To add insult to injury, here was a woman suggesting that she take on a very unladylike task for the good of the army. Officials were convinced that women were bad for army morale and would flee at the first sounds of battle. Her request, therefore, was refused.

Clara had no intention of taking no for an answer. However, a more pressing personal problem had suddenly arisen. Letters from her family in Massachusetts told her that her father was very ill. They urged her to come home.

Clara arrived in North Oxford in February, 1862. As soon as she arrived, she knew her father was dying. Despite her grief, when she wasn't with her father, she continued to swamp various government officials with pleading letters, asking for permission to go to the front. Captain Barton had been the person who first taught her the importance of service to her country. Even as he fought his last battle with life, she continued to fight hers.

Captain Barton died in March. With the other members of her family, Clara sadly attended his funeral. The only person missing was her brother Stephen. When the war began, communication between North and South became almost impossible. Clara had no idea whether Stephen was alive or dead. Her worry for him only added to her grief and her anxiety over the continuing struggle to obtain passes for the front.

It was a struggle that Clara finally won. Some time after the funeral, the government gave in and issued her a pass to attend the Army of the Potomac. Clara, overjoyed at the thought of bringing relief where it was most needed, began hastily to gather as many supplies as she could. In the upcoming months, she knew there would be a desperate need for her services.

By August, 1862 she had gathered three warehouses full of supplies. She made a trek to the Union camp in Fredericksburg, Virginia, to distribute them and was gratified to see that the soldiers' relief was immediate and overwhelming.

However, the pass Clara had been issued was meant to permit her simply to bring supplies. No one had thought that she would attempt to spend time at the actual battle sites. It is likely that no one would ever have given such permission had they known what was really on her mind.

Clara realized that she need not even apply for such permission. Instead, she simply used the pass she had been granted and persuaded officers and guards alike that it was a general pass for the front. No one questioned her. She probably would not have listened if they had. She was too busy focusing on ways of relieving the soldiers' suffering.

Clara's initiation into the horrors of war was the Second Battle of Manassas, sometimes called the Second Battle of Bull Run, fought in Virginia in September, 1862. Here she began to understand the size of the task that confronted her and the few other courageous helpers who had stepped forward to serve.

The Fairfax train station, close to the battle site, had been designated a makeshift Union hospital. Clara, arriving with wagonloads of supplies, heard the resounding rumble of the cannon in the distance and found three thousand men lying on straw that had been strewn on the cold station floor to serve as blankets.

She and Almira Fales, who accompanied her, worked in the tiny station for three days. Clara found old students and friends lying among the wounded. She tended dying men, men groaning in agony or screaming in pain, as well as men whose wounds were minor, who needed nothing more than food, drink and a kind word. She became used to the sight of bloody limbs, torn and mangled bodies and men whose faces were etched with the terror of battle.

As that battle wound down, a new battle developed. Little did Clara realize that within two days she would be back at Fairfax Station for still more difficult duty. At the very moment that she was wearily packing up her supplies to go home, Confederate general "Stonewall" Jackson turned on the tired Union troops retreating from Bull Run. Within hours, what began as a "cav-

A horse-drawn ambulance in use during the Civil War. For many soldiers, the long, jarring ride to the hospital was more dangerous than their wounds. Many died of hunger or thirst along the way. Clara Barton made sure that the wounded were given food and water before their difficult journey, saving the lives of many men.

alry charge in a cornfield" became the Battle of Chantilly. To make matters worse for Clara, she found that the medical supply wagons, carrying all manner of aid, had been left by the battle-weary soldiers on the road during their retreat from Bull Run. The exhausted surgeons were working with almost no supplies at all.

The combined battles brought Clara four days of non-stop work. She slept for two hours altogether during that time, and ate almost nothing at all. Yet despite her weariness and horror at what she had seen, she returned to Washington knowing she had found a niche for herself. It was a niche that history would never forget.

7

On the Battlefield

ONLY A FEW weeks after Clara's labors at Bull Run and Chantilly, she heard a rumor that a major battle was to be fought at Harper's Ferry. Clara was completely exhausted from the physical and the emotional burdens she had shouldered at the last battle, but that scrap of information readied her jagged nerves. She roused herself immediately and began to collect supplies once more.

The information turned out to be incorrect. There was no battle fought at Harper's Ferry. Clara by now, though, had staked her claim to follow the Army of the Potomac. Where they went, so would she.

Clara spent the first day out behind the supply wagons of the army. She was traveling, this time, with four surly soldiers who had been assigned to her by the War Department. None of the men knew who she was. None of them wanted to be part of an expedition led by a woman. When Clara asked for their help, they grumbled and muttered under their breath.

Clara recognized their resentment but believed it

would melt under the combination of firmness and kindness she had always shown her unruly students during her teaching days. Late in the afternoon, with the army trains still moving, the soldiers refused to obey Clara's instructions to continue the march. They said they were finished with their work for the day.

Clara said nothing. She simply sent them out to find wood for a fire and to tend the horses. When they returned, she was already cooking a hearty supper. She served them graciously despite their mutterings and smiled at them warmly throughout the meal. As with her unruly schoolboys, the soldiers could not resist her calm, sympathetic personality. From that evening forward, there was nothing they would not do for her.

Clara fretted because they had lost so much time in following the army wagons. What was worse, she knew that she and her supplies would arrive at the end of a long train of wagons, far behind the battle lines. If she were to save more lives and reach the wounded faster, she had to find a way to get to the head of the line. How could she do it?

As she lay on a makeshift army cot that night, Clara's mind worked busily. She remembered the military lessons her father had given her — the long discussions of tactics and strategies that she had committed to memory as a child. Suddenly, she knew exactly what she needed to do.

The answer was simple. Clara and her team had to pass the army, coming around the side in order to reach the head of the line by dawn. Quickly she roused her men and told them they were moving on. They were only half-awake, but Clara's tone of command was not to be ignored. Within the hour they were back on the jolting roads in pursuit of the army. Through the night and into the following morning they labored past the army train. By dawn of the next morning, exactly as Clara had calculated, their small train had circled around the army train and was positioned right behind the cannon, within sight of the battle itself.

The battle began that day along Antietam Creek. For one day 115,000 men fought each other across the lines of an eight-mile front. Almost forty thousand men died. It would become the first important Union victory, but it was one of the war's bloodiest and most horrifying battles.

Clara followed the cannon doggedly. When she saw Union forces being driven back, she directed her men to that spot. She found herself near a farmhouse, which had been hastily commandeered as a field hospital. The few army surgeons available were already working. Three hundred wounded men lay waiting their turn to be treated.

The doctors had almost no medical supplies at all. The medical supply wagon was far away, at the end of the supply train miles from their hospital. None of those vitally important supplies would reach them for hours. They were using corn leaves to bandage wounds. Their instruments were bloody from endless amputations. Through the smoke of the battle and the booming of the cannon they could hardly see or hear anything.

Clara scooped up piles of her own bandages and medicines and made her way to the porch. As she walked, the carnage around her made her shudder. She had never seen — and would never see again — scenes of such gore, such anguish, such horror. The twisted, bloody bodies and agonized cries of the dying haunted her dreams for the rest of her life.

The broiling sun was causing as much agony as the bullet wounds of the soldiers. Men lay almost on top of one another on the ground. The surgeons could not continue their work without some type of medication to ease the soldiers' pain. The grateful doctors accepted Clara's offerings and once more turned to the rows of patients bleeding in the fields.

Clara immediately commandeered the services of twelve healthy soldiers lingering on the porch. Together, they searched out wounded men and brought them to the farmhouse for treatment. Once there, Clara began her endless preparations of meals and administering of water and bandages.

Yet in this, the worst of all battles, even Clara was called on to do more than she had ever done previously. When her frightened male assistants, cowering from the bursting shells overhead, ran from the site where surgeons were operating, Clara steeled herself to step in and hold the rolling tables while the doctors cut off mangled limbs. There was no chloroform to ease the pain of the patients, who shrieked even as Clara held them. Yet she did not flinch from her grisly job. Her face remained calm and placid, as always. The wounded and terrified drew new strength from her unfailing peacefulness.

Clara even found it necessary to operate herself, without help from the surgeons. In the afternoon, a young boy who had a bullet lodged in his cheek asked her to cut out the ball in order to relieve the doctors of the necessity of treating him. Others, he told her, needed the doctors more than he did, but he was in terrible pain. Wouldn't she do him the favor of cutting out the bullet for him?

It was not something Clara felt sure she could do, despite her incredible efforts throughout the day. However, if her help would relieve the boy's suffering, she agreed to do it. A sergeant with wounds in both thighs assisted her by holding the patient's head still while Clara, penknife in hand, carefully cut out the bullet and washed and bandaged the boy's face. In later years she said that, while it was perhaps not a scientific operation, she hoped it was successful at least in relieving the patient's suffering.

It was a further shock, some hours later, to hear that the supplies she had carefully gathered were gone. The doctors and assistants had used every slice of bread, every cracker, every biscuit. They had nothing left to offer the hungry men but three boxes of wine. What should they do? Clara winced. All her scrounging for supplies seemed in vain. But what could she do except offer the wine and hope that the army supply wagons would get more to them later? Reluctantly, she gave orders to break open the boxes and pour out wine to the soldiers.

Two minutes later, she felt one of the greatest reliefs of her life. Clara had expected to see opened cartons of bottles packed for safety's sake in sawdust. However, the women who packed the wine had packed it instead in cornmeal. There was enough cornmeal for six kettlefuls of cornmeal mush, hearty fare to the hungry wounded men. Clara hunted in the farmhouse cellar and found three barrels of flour and a bag of salt left over by the Confederate Army, who had previously camped there. To the tired workers, the extra food was heaven-sent. Clara, practical as always, made a silent note to herself to bring more wagonfuls of supplies for the next battle.

The cornmeal, welcome as it was, also provided Clara an excellent lesson. From then on she would bring nothing to the battlefield that could not be used for the relief of the wounded. No matter how small an item, if it did not provide a necessary comfort, Clara decided, forever afterward, to leave it at home. Every inch of space in every relief carton was packed with what could provide the most relief. It was an instruction she passed on to her Red Cross workers down the years.

In the evening of that first day at Antietam, she brought welcome relief to the doctors, who had been working since daylight. One surgeon, savagely cursing the lack of supplies, was squinting in the gloom of the last flickering candle he had. When Clara offered him four boxes of kerosene lanterns, he dashed off to secure them without a word. Many years later, when she lectured in the Midwest about her wartime experiences, she told this story to her audience. A man rose to his feet.

"Madam," he declared, "I am that doctor. If I did not thank you then, I thank you now."

Antietam was the worst of Clara's wartime experiences. She never forgot the sounds of the battle that shrieked around her, nor could she ever erase the sights of the bloody, shattered men she tried to help. She remembered the frustration of the doctors, the lack of vital supplies, the inexperience and inability of some of her helpers.

It was also her greatest single test as a woman on the battlefield. Never again would she be so closely connected with the battle itself. It was at Antietam that Clara bent over one wounded man to offer him a cup of water. As she began to lift his head toward the cup, a bullet slashed through her sleeve and struck the soldier, killing him instantly. Clara, always aware of the many who needed her, quietly laid the dead man down and proceeded with her work. Yet that, too, was a moment she could never stop remembering.

The hell of Antietam brought out in Clara her most shining courage, her greatest strength. She could not afford to surrender to her own inner demons, if she was to bring the kind of aid she wished to bring to these men. Whatever the risk to herself, she would do the task she had set out to do. When she returned home, her first call was to the Assistant Quartermaster-General. She extracted from him a promise of more wagons on her next journey. Then she went home to bed.

Even as she slept, though, word of her heroism and dedication was already spreading. From that time forward, she was known in newspapers and dispatches as the "Angel of the Battlefield."

8

Following the Cannon

FROM ANTIETAM ON, it was Clara's policy to follow the cannon. She was always at her best in situations of emergency, even knowing that the artillery was firing nearby and that evacuation could be ordered at any moment. She always loved the feeling of security and purpose that enveloped her when she was around the army.

Throughout the war years, Clara was far from the only woman to serve the wounded. However, other women performed their service in hospitals, which were located away from the front, usually in large cities or nearby towns. They yielded to that common idea that women were too delicate to endure any kind of battle situations.

Many women preferred the leadership of nurses like Dorothea Dix. Miss Dix was the founder of a unit of hospital nurses who worked under strict supervision. She was intent on creating nurses who were both respectable and completely capable of handling the toughest nursing jobs. She required that ladies wishing to join her corps be unmarried and strong enough to turn a patient in bed without any assistance.

Clara found herself at odds with Miss Dix. Though both of them wanted to aid the wounded, Dorothea Dix had no intention of rendering any service on the battlefield. She was a hospital nurse. Also, she insisted on complete obedience from her nurses and laid down rigid rules regarding their conduct and performance.

Clara, who offered assistance in hospitals only when battles were not being fought, had spent too much time in emergency conditions to be able to conform to new regulations. She was a woman who had made her own rules during the feverish moments of battle. It was impossible for her to take the orders of another, no matter how well meaning or practical they might be. She also found the atmosphere of the city hospitals too stifling and almost too quiet. Clara was used to the clanging immediacy of the battlefield. Anything less jarred her.

Another problem began to surface as the war continued. By now Clara had achieved an astounding level of fame. Newspaper articles and letters written by soldiers and military surgeons told of her talent and dedication throughout the country. Wives and mothers across America were sending her supplies and letters pleading for information about missing sons and husbands.

This extraordinary attention from the public bothered certain people. Other dedicated nurses who also served faithfully, but in more commonplace ways in hospitals, felt Clara was robbing them of attention they rightfully deserved, too. As a result, they began to resent her fame and the notice given to her by the public.

Despite her war experiences, Clara remained a sensitive woman. She felt deeply the coldness shown her by some of the hospital nurses. When she thought about these feelings, she found her old depression reviving. The only way to stop it was to throw herself completely into her work and the suffering of others. Only in service, she realized, was she free of her old nagging feelings of failing.

Clara's life was taking on a new pace. When a battle ended and the wounded were cared for as completely as she could manage, she returned to her home in Washington. There, she rested and revived herself. She ate the food she had gone without during those long days and nights of nursing, cleaned and mended her limited wardrobe consisting of one simple battle dress that she used for her nursing work, and listened actively for news of the next battle.

Once she felt her health had returned sufficiently, usually in a day or so, she began to canvass for supplies once more. This meant long days of consultation with the Assistant Quartermaster-General, who became a staunch ally. The quartermaster of an army is the officer in charge of allotting supplies to the troops. Usually, hearing Clara's pleas and listings of the shortages she had to endure, the Assistant Quartermaster-General approved greater and greater amounts of supplies and transport for her. She had become, after all, one of the Union's greatest assets.

When word of new fighting came through, Clara was prepared to move at once. She gathered her supplies, stored them on wagons provided by the War Department, and began the torturous journey to the battle site.

All consideration of her own health and well-being was forgotten in the rush to reach the wounded.

Sometimes she caught up with the army before they actually met with the enemy. When that happened, Clara had the chance to become the companion of the soldiers, singing military songs with them, knitting as they drilled, and sharing their nightly campfires. The men adored her, and she returned their affection fully. Balancing her memories of the horror of smoke and battle were her warm feelings about the camaraderie of the soldiers and their gallantry toward her.

By now she regularly traveled with a minister, Reverend Cornelius Welles, to whom she had introduced the harsh realities of the battlefield. Though a somewhat fragile, unworldly man, he was quick to understand what was needed. As Clara bustled about her duties, cooking, nursing, and bathing the wounded, he assisted her and whispered prayers to the soldiers.

In late 1862, Union General Ambrose Burnside set into motion his plan to attack the Confederate capital city of Richmond, Virginia. Burnside was not anxious to fight the Confederate army, led by General Robert E. Lee. Therefore, he decided to bypass the rebel forces and come into Richmond by way of Fredericksburg. Clara, learning of the plan, went along with her supplies.

Fredericksburg sat on one side of the Rappahannock River. On the other side lay Richmond. If the Union forces could successfully cross the river, they could blaze into Richmond virtually unchallenged. Burnside planned to have Union engineers erect temporary bridges so that they could make the crossing.

However, Confederate snipers lay in wait on the other side of the river. As the engineers began their important work, they were shelled by gunmen they could not even see. Burnside, an unimaginative man, was unable to change his plan to adapt to the new circumstances. He insisted that the engineers continue their work, though they were being killed almost as fast as they could build the bridges.

Clara remained on the banks of the river, away from the shelling, until she received a short and bloody note from a Union surgeon across the river: "Come to me — your place is here." Without a glance backward, she stepped onto the first rickety bridge, hearing the shells burst around her as she hurried toward Richmond.

A kind officer helped Clara down from the bridge at the other side. As his hand grasped hers, a bullet sliced between them, cutting off a piece of her skirt and his coattail. Less than half an hour later, as she began work at the hospital, he was brought to her — dead.

Twelve thousand men died as a result of Burnside's tragic mistake. During that time, Clara worked as she always worked. With the coming of cold weather, a new sorrow added to the plight of the wounded. Those left on the fields were not only exposed to the cold winds but to the freezing ground. Clara found many whose skins were now frostbitten, whose bodies were frozen fast to the frozen mud. Exposure was killing the wounded as fast as the bullets.

An old, gracious house, named Lacy House, became the hospital site for the Union wounded. As she moved from room to room, Clara's sympathetic eyes ached at the sight of men who, lacking space on beds and floors, were crammed, two and three at a time, into china shelves and stuck under table legs. Nonetheless, she remained as steely and firm as ever. Each wounded man must be nourished, bathed and comforted. Each wounded man must be removed to safety.

Clara kept her cheerful countenance until the end of the battle, when her supplies were exhausted. Most of the wounded had been removed to hospitals in the North. She no longer needed to maintain her smile for the troops. On her return to Washington, she sat down on the floor of her room and wept.

In the spring of 1863 things were changing again for Clara. Her brother David had been appointed a quartermaster in the army and sent to Port Royal at Hilton Head, South Carolina. The Eighteenth Army Corps would soon be blasting the nearby Confederate city of Charleston. They needed to be certain of an unbroken flow of provisions from Washington.

Clara went with David to Hilton Head. Though the bombardment began the very day she arrived, on April 7, she, herself, saw no action for awhile. The army's plans proceeded slowly. For the first time since the onset of the war, Clara had plenty of time to enjoy herself among the military personnel gathered at Hilton Head. She spent mornings horseback riding with Colonel John J. Elwell of Cleveland, Ohio, who became a particularly close friend. She enjoyed the company of Frances Dana Gage and her daughter Mary, who worked among the free blacks living on the Sea Islands, just off Hilton Head. She was especially delighted to dine often with Captain Samuel T. Lamb, an old friend whose father had been the Barton family doctor for many years.

Yet this period of grace and peace, welcome as it was, did not keep Clara from her purpose. While the rest of the world was suffering, she felt guilty enjoying the kind of innocent pastimes that she had abandoned when the war began.

There was a return to action when the siege of Charleston began in July, 1863. Unlike battles which are fought and won or lost, a siege is a slow, draining process marked less by fighting than by endurance. Clara worked with the wounded in the first days, but found herself unnecessary as the slow waiting wore on. She returned to Hilton Head, accompanied by Elwell, who had been wounded on the beach during the first day of the Union takeover. Clara nursed him through the crisis but now even he no longer needed her care. Her services and special talents were not called for in this type of warfare.

Moreover, her hard-won supplies and the respect she had commanded from the army were both wearing thin. Army surgeons took for themselves the brand-new sturdy tents she had brought with her. They claimed it was their privilege to seize any property which would help them. Clara's claim to the goods was ignored. In addition, her brother David, an inexperienced man who had not sought the position of quartermaster, was not performing his duties with any great skill. The contempt he recieved because of his mistakes spilled over onto Clara. Through no fault of her own, she was once more making enemies. She decided to leave South Carolina for a place where she could be useful.

General Ulysses S. Grant now took over command of the Army of the Potomac. Grant was a ruthless and steely man who would sacrifice any number of troops for a victory. He became famous in the North after his campaign in Spotsylvania County, Virginia, where casualties ran into the thousands.

Clara rushed to Fredericksburg, where the wounded were being brought in by ambulance. Rain poured down into the red Virginia clay, while hundreds of wagons stuck fast in the mud, unable to move. The wounded lay exposed to the pounding rain, even as the wagons jolted them in their attempts to get free of the mud and onto clear roads.

Clara did not waste time trying to get the men to shelter. She cooked kettles of cornmeal mush, took as many crackers as she could carry, and stepped into the mud. Slogging from wagon to wagon, she fed the men and covered them as best she could to protect them from the rain.

When Clara learned that there were privately owned houses that could have been used to shelter the wounded in Fredericksburg, her first question was why these homes were not opened to the men. The answer was that the military had refused to order the homes opened. High-ranking officers felt that no one in Fredericksburg should be ordered to share their homes with common dirty foot soldiers. So the homeowners stayed in their roomy comfortable homes, while the soldiers lay on bare, bloody floors in an old run-down hotel, desperate for food and water. No one but Clara had given them any kind of nourishment for days.

Clara was furious. She returned to Washington immediately and caught the ear of Henry Wilson, an old friend who was now head of the Senate Military Committee. At two o'clock the next morning, an investigating committee from Washington set off for Fredericksburg. They arrived eight hours later and examined the conditions Clara had described. By noon, the wounded were being moved into the large, gracious homes and fed from the city's own stores.

Meanwhile, more personal troubles arose. Clara's brother Stephen, whose whereabouts were unknown when the war began, had been arrested by Union officers as a member of the Confederacy. He tried to tell them he was a Union sympathizer, but they did not believe him. By this time he was a sick, old and broken man. His business was in ruins. The three thousand dollars that remained of his fortune was taken from him upon his arrest.

Clara, using her political influence, managed to get him released from prison and restored to him the money that had been stolen. But Stephen was now a dying man. Clara used her own last reserves of strength to nurse him.

The effort was futile. Stephen died in March, 1865. A month later, General Robert E. Lee surrendered his army to General Grant at Appomattox Court House in Virginia. The great war was over.

Clara was relieved that the bloody war was finished. As she surveyed the remains of her own life, though, a faint regret began to creep into her thoughts. For four years she had been on call in the most dramatic manner. She had served in every possible condition and often against extreme odds. She had loved every moment of her work.

Now, at forty-three, a part of her life was over for good. There were no more battlefields to serve on. The sudden peace had left a gaping hole in her life. She had no idea what she was going to do next.

9

Andersonville and Beyond

I N APRIL, 1865, as the country began mending its wounds after four years of war, Clara made her way back to the Patent Office in Washington. She assumed she would simply pick up the threads of her old job once more. She found, though, that the war had made an indelible impact on her life, as it had so many others. She could not go back to the quiet life she had known before. She would soon be called on to undertake a new responsibility that sprang directly from her years of military service.

From the very beginning of her nursing days, Clara had received frantic letters of inquiry from wives and mothers. They knew nothing about the fate of their sons and husbands in the army. Did Clara know where they were and whether or not they were all right?

Throughout the war, Clara had done her best to learn what she could about these missing men. The War Department had set up no specific mechanism to trace those missing in battle. Clara knew from her worry over Stephen exactly how frantic a woman could be about a missing loved one. Whenever she could, she tried to help locate these men.

When the war ended on April 9, 1865, however, there were still thousands of men missing. Clara was very concerned that each soldier be accounted for in some way. She went to President Abraham Lincoln for permission to assume responsibility for tracing these men.

Despite her fame, to the White House guards Clara was just another woman seeking favors from the President. Patiently, persistently, she made her way to the President's home for three days in a row, carefully dressed in her gown and hat, asking politely for a few minutes with Mr. Lincoln. Finally, she was admitted.

President Lincoln heartily approved Clara's plan to find the missing men. He wrote a personal letter requesting that all information and inquiries about these soldiers be directed to Clara. This letter was published in newspapers all over the country. At the president's direction, the War Department arranged for Clara to have a sturdy tent and a few hundred dollars' worth of postage. This meager office was set up at Annapolis, Maryland, where thousands of soldiers were discharged from the Union Army. It was Lincoln's last service for Clara. He was assassinated on April 14, 1865, less than a week after the war ended.

With the publication of the president's letter, Clara found herself the recipient of hundreds of inquiries, practically overnight. Not all the letters were from families writing about missing relatives. Clara found to her relief that many were instructions from soldiers who had buried a comrade and marked his grave if there was any type of marker available. The work was slow, difficult and heartbreaking. It seemed as though the whereabouts of thousands of men would never be known at all. However, Clara's persistence led to the positive location of eight thousand missing men.

Then a young man appeared with a document that eased Clara's burden and provided thousands of new names for her files. The man was Dorence Atwater, a former Union soldier who had at one time been imprisoned in the Confederate camp at Andersonville, Georgia. Andersonville was the most notorious of the Confederate prisoner-of-war camps. Located deep in a Georgia backwoods swamp, it housed thousands of Union prisoners in a wooden stockade barely adequate for several hundred. The Confederate army had little enough food for its own soldiers. It fed its prisoners on whatever was left. The Union soldiers ate meals consisting mostly of corn or potatoes, often half-rotted. Blankets were in scarce supply, as were uniforms or clothing of any sort.

The Union soldiers died by the hundreds, left to starve or freeze or shiver in the grip of fevers and scurvy. Dorence Atwater saw this terrible situation first hand. The Confederate commander of Andersonville had ordered Atwater to work with him as a clerk of sorts. Because the young soldier had a clear, legible handwriting, the commander asked him to record the deaths of the prisoners on a camp list.

Atwater was outraged by the numbers of the dead, sometimes seven hundred per week. He firmly believed that the officials at Andersonville were deliberately starving and torturing their prisoners. So at night, when he had written down the day's records for the com-

81

mander, he copied them onto a secret list for himself. The list remained hidden in his coat lining while he was there. When he was freed, he brought the list home with him. When several government officials dismissed his attempts to gain their attention, Atwater sought an introduction to Clara and presented the list to her.

When Clara looked at it, she was stunned. Atwater had listed fourteen thousand names! This remarkable document would go a long way toward clearing up the mystery of the missing men.

Clara set to work at once. The officials who had dismissed Atwater's pleas could not dismiss hers. She insisted that the government assign a party to return to Andersonville and create a proper cemetery with graves that were clearly marked. Finally, a military party was assembled. Clara and Atwater accompanied them to Georgia.

The first sight of Andersonville stunned the workers. Accustomed as they were to seeing awful sights during the war, this dreadful ruin still turned their stomachs. They saw the pitiful holes in the ground where prisoners had tried to tunnel their way to freedom. They saw the filthy tin cups which held the water the prisoners drank to stay alive. Worst of all, they saw the mass graves where bodies had been tossed, one on top of another, and shoveled over with dirt.

For several weeks, the party labored to rebuild the ruin into a place of some dignity for the dead. Clara found herself at odds with the military commander of the expedition, Captain James B. Moore. Moore believed himself to be the unquestioned leader of the group, though it was Clara's initiative and Atwater's list that had made the journey possible. Clara, who felt this trek to be an extension of her work in tracing missing men, believed she was the leader of the force.

Her relations with Captain Moore began with a misunderstanding about transportation and grew worse as the weeks went by. Moore refused to give Clara any more than the barest courtesies. Clara, who felt the snub keenly, made no move to defend herself. As was her usual policy, she threw herself instead into her work.

She spent her time nursing the few inmates left at Andersonville, trying to build up their strength for the long journey home. She also received visits from curious former slaves in the area who had heard about her. Many were uneducated and unsure of what their freedom actually meant. Many were being taken advantage of by their former owners and other dishonest whites. Clara did her best to help them understand their position. She also sought government assistance for them when she returned to Washington.

The cemetery at Andersonville was officially dedicated on August 17, 1865. Clara was chosen to hoist the American flag over the former prison. When the ceremony was over, she left the site, hoping to avoid Captain Moore for the rest of her life.

That hope was in vain, however. At the end of the month, Clara learned that Dorence Atwater had been arrested for larceny. The list of the Andersonville dead that Atwater had presented to the government was missing. Atwater admitted to taking it, because he believed it was rightfully his. He had temporarily permitted the government's use of it while they were erecting the cemetery, but now he wanted it back. The government insisted that the document belonged to them.

Captain Moore testified for the prosecution during Atwater's court-martial. Moore had been in charge of securing the list, and its loss was an embarrassment to him. He was anxious for its return to clear this blemish on his record. As a result, Atwater was convicted of larceny, fined three hundred dollars, dishonorably discharged from the military and sentenced to eighteen months in prison.

Clara, who had not fought Moore on her own behalf, now took up Atwater's cause with her usual fervor. She was upset that Atwater was detained in the Old Capitol Prison, where conditions were wretched. She smuggled in food and money to the prisoner and made efforts to examine the transcript of the court-martial. What she read convinced her that Atwater had been railroaded by men like Moore, who were seeking to protect their own interests.

This time, however, Clara was not strong enough to effect a change. Her health was once more breaking down. She had no allies in the military court. In the end, to her sorrow, she saw Atwater go off to prison in irons. He was released after serving two months on the order of President Andrew Johnson, who freed all military offenders not held on assault charges.

As fall turned into winter, Clara's personal finances became a new worry. She was no longer on the rolls of the Patent Office. She had no source of income. In addition, she had spent a good deal of her own money on the correspondence for the missing men. In February

1866, Congress voted her a reimbursement of fifteen thousand dollars in bonds.

However, Clara knew she would need some sort of steady income in order to pursue her work to its completion. Her friend Frances Gage suggested that she take up lecturing. Her war experiences, the trek to Andersonville, her hunt for the missing men and the recent heartbreak over Atwater would all provide what Gage thought was excellent material. Also, she pointed out to Clara that she would now be able to tell her side of the story about her stormy relationship with Captain Moore, whom she suspected had slandered her name. It could also not hurt to meet some of the people for whom she was currently no more than a legend.

Clara finally agreed. She began a lecture tour in November 1866, charging seventy-five to a hundred dollars per lecture. When she spoke on behalf of soldiers' charities, she refused to accept a fee.

The lectures themselves sparkled with the drama that Clara herself had experienced. Her audiences, often small-town citizens seeing her for the first time, were solidly impressed with her descriptions of military life and the horrors of the battlefield. Clara found herself touring the New England area for two years. Finally, in a tiny Maine town in the spring of 1868, her voice gave out again.

Weary, aching and once more fighting her recurring depressions, Clara returned to North Oxford to consult with her old family physician, Dr. Fuller. She was tired and disinterested in her work. The correspondence had slowed to a trickle. She had found all the men she thought she could expect to find. A clerk could run the office from now on.

Dr. Fuller told her simply that she needed a change of scene and new projects to occupy her mind. He advised a long journey to a warm climate. Clara decided to make a trip to Europe, and chose her sister Sally to accompany her.

Several months later, having set her affairs in order, she and Sally set off for the Old World hoping that the new scenes would lift Clara's spirits. She did not know, when she stepped onto the shore at Glasgow, Scotland, that she was just beginning her greatest adventure of all.

With the end of the Civil War in 1865, Clara Barton returned to Washington D.C., ready to take up a new cause. This portrait by famous photographer Mathew Brady was taken at the beginning of her mission to locate the thousands of soldiers who remained missing.

10

The Red Cross

CLARA HOPED THAT Europe would bring back her flagging energy once more. She was forty-seven years old and completely worn down with the stresses of the past few years. She wanted desperately to find someplace or something that would revive her will to serve again. Her doctor's orders had been explicit: Take three years off and do nothing. Even as she promised the doctor that she would obey him, however, Clara knew that doing nothing would be harmful to her.

Still, when she and Sally arrived in Glasgow in the fall of 1869, Clara was too weak to do anything but submit to her sister's care. All her life she suffered from seasickness, and the rocking of the ship on which they crossed the Atlantic Ocean further sapped her strength. She was looking forward to a vacation of calm and peace.

To her surprise, Clara found she liked Scotland. Though the climate was harsh, the towns and fields were beautiful and the skies were clear. She and Sally wandered about the old castles and the colorful countryside for two weeks, then continued on to London.

In London, Sally bid Clara goodbye. Her children needed her at home. Clara, who was beginning to feel stronger and more alert with the passing days, continued alone to Paris for a short time, then to Geneva, Switzerland.

Here at last she saw familiar faces. The American diplomat to Geneva was Charles Upton, whom Clara had known since her early days in Washington. Upton and his wife welcomed her warmly to Geneva. She found a hearty reception also from the Swiss family of Jules Golay, a young soldier she had met during her rounds in the hospitals in America. The Golays insisted that she stay with them during her visit to Geneva.

Unfortunately, while the Swiss air was fresh and clear, it was also bitterly cold. As fall turned into winter, the wind blowing across the lake became harsher. Clara spent her time huddled in bed trying to escape the cold. Soon, deciding she couldn't recover her strength in such cold, she had to move on to Corsica, an island off Italy. Here she hoped to find warmer temperatures.

Corsica did provide sunshine, but Clara found the food greasy and inedible. The various inns where she stayed were dirty, unkempt and unfriendly. Restless, unhappy and lonely, she moved from place to place, hoping that the next hotel would be more hospitable. Everywhere she went she was disappointed. She returned to Switzerland as soon as the spring, and warmth, arrived.

It was a beautiful spring in Geneva, and Clara reveled in its cleanliness and friendliness. The Uptons invited her to stay with them, and Clara quickly regained her health in the sunshine and luxury of the Uptons' lovely home. However, with the return of her strength came the inevitable feeling of depression. As she walked about the grounds, she was gnawed by the lack of purpose in her days. Despite the doctor's orders, she could not just do nothing for any length of time without becoming seriously upset. She knew she needed an outlet for her pent-up energies.

During her earlier visit to Geneva, Clara had received a courtesy call from a small band of men identifying themselves as representatives of the International Convention of Geneva, called the Red Cross. Led by Dr. Louis Appia, they explained to the interested American woman that theirs was an organization prepared to offer aid to those afflicted by war.

The organization had been founded by a young Swiss man, Jean Henri Dunant, who in 1859 witnessed a battle between the French and the Austrians in Solferino, Italy, in which forty thousand men were killed or wounded. Dunant saw the suffering of the wounded and the terrible shortages of the simplest supplies. He knew that saving many of them was a matter of securing both provisions and assistance from qualified volunteers. Swiftly, he gathered as many supplies as he could scrounge and pressed village women into service as nurses. Like Clara, he worked for days on end directing operations and ministering to the wounded himself.

When Dunant finished his battlefield work, the carnage continued to haunt him. What could he do, he wondered, to prevent such terrible shortages in the future?

The answer was to found a relief organization that would stock provisions against emergencies on a year-round basis. Warehouses filled with supplies would be ready when disaster struck, and volunteers would be prepared to step in at a moment's notice. Aid would be offered to anyone who required it, regardless of nationality or beliefs. All wounded were to be treated the same.

Dunant joined forces with a prominent Swiss man named Gustave Moynier to promote the new society. By February 1863 they were able to call a convention of sixteen European countries. Within eighteen months the Treaty of Geneva, outlining the basic beliefs Dunant had set forth, was launched. Eleven countries signed the treaty at once. By the time Louis Appia and his band of men called on Clara, thirty-two countries had already signed the treaty.

In honor of Dunant, a Swiss citizen, the new organization chose for its emblem the reverse of the Swiss flag which boasted a white cross on a red background. The emblem of the new relief society was a red cross on a white background. The group was therefore named the Red Cross.

To Clara's amazement, Appia told her the United States had been approached to sign the treaty and refused three times. Did she, as an American, know why this could be?

Clara did not know, as she had never heard of the Red Cross and knew nothing about America's consideration of the treaty. However, she began to read the Red Cross literature Appia left for her. It was fascinating. Here, finally, was a practical solution to the problems she herself had encountered during the Civil War. What an extraordinary help it would be, Clara thought as she read, not to scrounge for supplies or assistants when a disaster occurred. It could certainly save time — and lives — to have stores of provisions and trained volunteers ready whenever a wartime emergency came up.

Only a few weeks later, in July 1870, the Franco-Prussian War began. The French were afraid that Germany was becoming supreme in its military and political power in Europe. Therefore, as an excuse to fight Germany, France declared war on Prussia, along with its allies, including Germany.

Clara plunged into relief work immediately. She joined the Red Cross workers headed for the storehouses of supplies located in Basel, Switzerland. Clara gasped as she saw the mountains of clean, fresh provisions tagged and ready to be used at once. Her first glimpse of these storehouses was enough to convince her that the Red Cross was making an extraordinary contribution to mankind. She knew she would have to become involved in furthering its cause in America.

Now she was involved in the same kind of service she had given during the Civil War. It was exhilarating to be once more in the dramatic rush of wartime events. Clara felt her depression blow away like a mist in a strong wind. She was needed. Her energies were once again directed toward a single goal. She joined the stream of workers on their way to the wounded, proudly wearing the Red Cross badge on her arm.

Wars in Europe were not the same as in America. Europeans had stricter standards about the nature of their battlefields and hospitals. Clara was absolutely forbidden to work on the battlefield, as she had done so often before, and she was refused permission to work in the hospitals, as well.

Clara was taken aback by the wall of refusals that blocked her way, but her energy was too high to be spent in waiting for dispatches from the front. With her quick, practical mind, Clara had noticed many poor women in the town of Strasbourg, France, where German artillery had left a bustling village in ruins. Hundreds of casualties lay in hospital wards, while others, unharmed but penniless, wandered the streets numbly.

Clara knew that part of rebuilding life after a disaster was rebuilding faith in one's own ability to work. From her own experience, she knew that loss of faith in one's self was a terrible fate. Therefore, she founded the "workrooms for women" in Strasbourg and brought in many women whose lives had been shattered by the German bombardment.

The workrooms were based on a system that a woman named Josephine Griffing had used in Washington to help freed slaves. They provided an environment and materials with which the women could sew new, inexpensive clothing that would then be donated to homeless war refugees. The women themselves were paid for their work by contributions Clara collected. Almost at once, she began to notice a lift in the spirits of these women, who were proud of the work they produced and pleased with the wages they were paid. Their wages would, in turn, provide food and shelter for their own hungry children. Clara saw that in the return to normal, productive employment, the town struggled harder to raise itself up than it might have if simply given charity without anything expected of its citizens in return. This policy of work for pay would be the foundation of the relief Clara would offer for the rest of her life.

Clara had begun the workroom project with sixty-seven women in the fall of 1870. By January of 1871, over two hundred women delivered more than fifteen hundred individual pieces of clothing each week. Every scrap of available material was used, whether for a child's mitten or a colorful vest for a grown man. By June, she knew that the project could continue without her. She traveled on to Paris, which had been devastated by the German army.

Clara remained in Paris for some months doing relief work, but at nearly fifty, she was no longer the young woman she once was. The months of hard work began to take their toll, and once more her health interfered with her ability to serve. Her eyes were so weak that she kept them bandaged and away from strong light. Her depression over the smallest details of her life kept her from concentrating for long on any single project. Her friends agreed that she would be better off resting in London during the spring of 1872.

The illness did not subside. Despite the friends who offered their services to her, Clara felt she was a useless old woman. She was embarrassed that she, who had nursed so many, now needed nursing from someone else. Her condition was still grave a year later, when she learned that her sister Sally was ill.

Anxious to be at Sally's bedside, Clara roused herself from her sickbed. She knew that her sister needed her, and she hurried to pack her bags for the journey home.

As she threw together the remnants of her life in Europe, she did not realize just how much she was bringing back to America with her.

As she sailed for New York in September 1873, she had, packed securely in her baggage, the pamphlets and papers she had accumulated in her dealings with the Red Cross. These papers would be the foundation on which she would build the remaining years of her life. They would also change the course of American history.

11

Bringing the Red Cross
to America

CLARA HAD SUMMONED all her remaining strength for the journey home so that she could nurse Sally, who was dying of cancer. By the time she arrived in America, however, her own condition was so grave that Sally would not let Clara tire herself by nursing her. Instead, Clara spent her time resting, hoping to regain her health once more. When Sally died in May, 1874, Clara was too ill even to attend the funeral.

Clara was now fifty-two years old. She was still haunted by bouts of bronchitis, weak eyes and recurring depression. There were days when she did not have the energy to get out of bed. She tried to fight against the weakness she felt constantly, but it was a fight she could not win alone.

To add to her melancholy, Clara continued to notice that the service which had brought her such acclaim from strangers and foreigners had brought no recognition at all from her own family. In fact, her relatives through the years had withheld any praise for her achievements, a fact that hurt Clara, who had always sought their respect. It seemed now as though nothing she did would ever earn that respect. Her family, she wrote unhappily, rather than being proud of her, had told her she was "in danger of being spoiled like a vain forward child and must be held in check." This in particular contributed to many days of black misery for Clara.

She began to consult doctors about her condition, hoping to find someone who could give her back the vigor and drive she used to have. Nothing seemed to work. Finally, a friend suggested that she look into a sanitarium in Dansville, New York.

"Our Home on the Hillside," as the doctors called the Dansville sanitarium, was cheerful, peaceful and comforting. Patients were treated as guests, housed in little cottages and fed good, wholesome meals. They were encouraged to participate in all kinds of activities, from quiet walks to small theatrical productions they staged themselves.

Clara arrived in Dansville in March 1876, after over a year of serious illness. Within a short time, she began to revive noticeably. The atmosphere and the kind attention of the doctors agreed with her. Several of the other patients became good friends. Clara afterward became so fond of Dansville that she bought a home and lived there for the next ten years.

In her year-long stay, Clara had once more regained her health. She felt fresher and more energetic than at any time since the war years. Naturally, her recovery led to restlessness. What should she do with her life now that she was healthy again?

The answer was the International Red Cross. Now was the time to find the answer to the question of why the United States had repeatedly refused to acknowledge the Treaty of Geneva. Further, Clara reasoned, it was important to establish a Red Cross in America to deal with American disasters. It would be a serious and difficult endeavor, especially for someone just recovering from a serious illness, but once more she took up someone else's fight.

Clara had maintained a correspondence with Dr. Appia, who first introduced her to the principles of the organization. He made sure Clara was appointed the American representative of the Red Cross, and throughout her years of recovery at Dansville, they kept in close touch.

At this time, Clara also met Julian Hubbell, a young man who would be a close friend for the remaining years of her life. Coincidentally, Hubbell lived in Dansville himself. He had read a great deal about Clara's work on the battlefield during the Civil War. Though he had not been old enough to serve during the war, Clara's exploits fired his imagination. When he found out she was living in Dansville he lost no time in calling on her. His admiration of her and dogged devotion to her causes helped to soothe her during many times of criticism by others. He would become one of the most important figures in the latter part of her life.

Clara's mind was beginning to revolve on the question of bringing the Red Cross to America. She would need a great deal of help and support, and she knew it. Hubbell was anxious to serve her in any way he could. When he asked what he could do for the organization, she answered promptly, "Become a doctor." On the strength of those words alone, Hubbell immediately made plans to do so. Later, when he had received his medical degree, he would go on to become the first field agent of the American Red Cross.

Meanwhile, Clara needed to determine exactly what had gone wrong when the International Red Cross approached America for its support. Why did the United States refuse to become involved?

To take up the fight directly, Clara returned to Washington. She was well enough to journey from office to office, asking questions but receiving few satisfactory answers. Day after day she wrote to government officials, called personally and tried to break through the stone wall of political indifference. Many of the men she had known before in government service were either dead or retired. There were new faces now, and a lot of them had little respect or interest in Clara Barton.

Still, Clara persisted. Finally, she began to piece together the reasons that America had refused to become part of the Treaty of Geneva. The Treaty specifically stated that it was operating as a relief society in *wartime* emergencies.

That one qualifying word re-opened the wounds that America had suffered in its own recent Civil War. Americans were fed up with war. Should the Europeans want to fight each other, they told themselves, it's none of our business. We don't want to be dragged into their battles, even if we're only supplying aid.

Representatives reading the provisions of the Treaty did not see the potential in storehouses of supplies ready for distribution at the first sign of disaster. They read only the word *wartime* and refused to read any further. The International Red Cross had set up no provisions for peacetime emergencies.

Clara now understood the government's refusal to sign the Treaty. Her own battle experiences had convinced her that war was an ugly, tragic business. However, this did not deter her from pointing out to Washington officials the importance of an organization that offered relief from peacetime disasters, as well. While war was certainly a disaster, there were many other kinds. Floods, droughts, fires and avalanches could also wreak havoc in the lives of people who were unprepared for them. An American Red Cross could assure swift help to people who needed food, shelter and medical care right away.

Still, the government refused. Clara patiently researched American history through the years. She discovered that at least once a year Americans in some part of the country had suffered a disaster such as tidal waves, hurricanes, earthquakes or epidemics. While none of these was a wartime disaster, each brought with it great suffering that could have been relieved by a national organization that was prepared for it. When she pointed this out to the government, it fell on deaf ears.

Clara turned to her friends and to organizations with whom she had been identified through the years. The Grand Army of the Republic (G.A.R.) was a society of Civil War veterans of the Union Army. They had embraced Clara as one of their own ever since her wartime service. Now she asked them to endorse the formation of an American Red Cross. They did.

This led to speaking engagements in which Clara summoned all the speechmaking tricks she had learned in her early Washington days. She pounded on lecterns, she coaxed, she spoke in whispers of the tragedies she had seen. Her lectures began to attract newspaper attention.

This eventually attracted the notice of President James Garfield, who was much impressed with Clara's sincerity and passion. He wrote her to suggest that she meet with his Secretary of State, James G. Blaine. Blaine listened sympathetically and sent her on to various cabinet members, including Secretary of War Robert Lincoln, the oldest son of the late president. Everyone in the Garfield cabinet seemed to be in agreement with Clara about the necessity of signing the Treaty of Geneva. After a round of such meetings, Clara came away glowing. She was certain that this time she would get the support she needed from the government.

Clara felt once more utterly defeated when President Garfield was shot in the summer of 1881. On his death, his entire cabinet would be replaced by other men. Who knew whether the new cabinet would be sympathetic to her?

Clara returned home to Dansville to regroup. There she was met with a wonderful surprise. The citizens of Dansville believed wholeheartedly in her and in all she was trying to accomplish. They asked her to help them form a local chapter of the Red Cross in their town.

Clara was delighted to do so. On August 22, 1881, she and several town leaders proclaimed Dansville the first local auxiliary of the Red Cross. Annual dues for each member was twenty-five cents. Clara supplied the group with literature and practical suggestions. They in turn raised funds to buy supplies and stored them in town, ready for any emergency that should strike. Within a few months Syracuse and Rochester, two large cities in upstate New York, founded their own chapters.

The effectiveness of this effort was tested almost at once. In mid-September, drought, hot winds, and careless behavior on the part of residents created a massive forest fire in Michigan. Firefighters were overwhelmed by the acres of land burning. Their equipment was hardly adequate to fight such a huge blaze. There were nearly five hundred lives lost, and the damage throughout the area was devastating. Fifteen hundred families lost their homes and possessions in the blaze.

Immediately, the Dansville Red Cross chapter began to organize donations for the survivors of the fire. Clara sent Julian Hubbell, then studying at the University of Michigan, to survey the damage and report back to her, while she remained in Dansville to organize relief. Hubbell also received and distributed the packages sent from the Dansville chapter. While both Rochester and Syracuse had contributed large sums of money to the effort, Hubbell found that private donors in Michigan were far more organized in their own relief efforts. After a few weeks, Hubbell concluded that the Red Cross had done all they could do. He quietly withdrew from the fire site.

Clara was disappointed that the Red Cross had not received more attention, which would have been excellent publicity in her campaign to be recognized by the American government. However, she was content that the local chapters had sprung to order so quickly and been so generous in their help. At least the Michigan fire proved that there was a necessity for a permanent organization to minister to disaster victims.

Chester A. Arthur became president of the United States in the fall of 1881. Clara watched his inauguration with mixed feelings. She did not know whether he would continue the support that the Garfield administration had given her. It was a wonderful surprise when she found that he would.

Much to Clara's dismay, other rival organizations began springing up. A group called the Blue Anchor claimed the same kind of relief policies as the Red Cross. Their continuing attempts to secure government recognition upset Clara greatly. She had spent years in the nurturing of this dream. She did not want it to die because another group was competing against hers.

In February of 1882, she called on the assistant to the Secretary of State. To her amazement, he handed her a softbound book containing the Treaty of Geneva, which would shortly be placed before Congress as a document to be signed. Clara cried openly as she looked down at the pages of the Treaty for which she had worked for five long years. On March 16, the Treaty was officially ratified by Congress.

It was a triumph for Clara. Throughout years of bureaucracy, politics and fighting, Clara had gotten increasingly frustrated. Yet she had persisted and finally won.

At the age of sixty, she was named the first president of the American Red Cross.

12

Relief From Disaster

THE BATTLE WAS far from over. The establishment of the American Red Cross and its recognition by the government was just the first step. Now Clara faced the monumental job of building the tiny organization into a full-fledged, smoothly functioning operation. Her fight on behalf of others was growing in its scope.

In the first year of its existence, the Red Cross bore its first disasters. The two floodings of the Mississippi River, which swept away whole houses and families and destroyed entire crops. There were few deaths in the floods, but the survivors were destitute. Without their crops, they had no way of earning a living. Julian Hubbell, now in medical school, represented the Red Cross on the scene. Meanwhile, local chapters springing up all over the country sent all manner of aid to the ruined farmers.

The Red Cross also involved itself in other relief efforts such as aiding the victims of the tornado that swept through Louisiana and Mississippi in 1883. However, Clara determined that the organization should offer aid only in cases of extreme distress or disasters of national importance. Clara knew that the resources of her struggling foundation were very slim. She needed to guard them carefully. She herself put it this way: "We must hold ourselves dear and rare, gather and husband our resources, and be ready to move like the winds when the true moment comes." Ever afterward, the Red Cross policy was to survey the disaster first, before deciding whether or not to offer relief.

Clara herself struggled with the day-to-day work. Now in her sixties, she dared not work less than an eighteen-hour day in order to keep up with the correspondence and handle the administrative details. In times of disaster, she made long, rough journeys to the emergency sites herself. When she was actively engaged in those efforts, her work day was often twenty hours long.

The lessons she had learned under fire at Antietam became her watchword in her Red Cross work. Only items that would supply practical relief could be taken to a disaster site. Food, clothing and practical comforts were always her first consideration in relief packages. Other, less necessary items could be shipped in later.

Her firmest policy was that disaster victims needed more psychological boosting than they did charity. Like the Strasbourg workrooms for women that she started in France, Clara's efforts in emergencies were bent toward helping people begin to help themselves again. She believed that simply handing out provisions to disaster victims led to their unhealthy dependence on other people. When people were producing their own necessities once more, Clara felt, they were likelier to recover faster from a calamity and grow stronger in the process.

This policy is a tribute to Clara's farsightedness. It is also rooted in her own personality. She knew from personal experience that she was happy only when she was busy and active. Left alone without a purpose, she fell into depression and self-doubt. In order to avoid the same thing happening to disaster victims, she encouraged her relief workers to pack their bags as soon as possible after they had rendered emergency aid. This may have been the Red Cross's greatest gift of all.

Clara's work was not limited simply to the Red Cross, however. In 1883, she also accepted the position of superintendent at the Massachusetts Reformatory Prison for Women, in Sherborn, Massachusetts. The work required a woman with skills and a warm, caring attitude toward the prisoners she would be overseeing.

Clara began her service at Sherborn in May. To her surprise, many of the women prisoners knew of her from her wartime service and respected and admired her. Discipline was not a problem. Like the students in her teaching days, the prisoners responded to Clara's warmth and kindness. However, there were episodes of infighting and jockeying for position among other officials at the Reformatory. Clara felt unhappily isolated since her agreement with the governor required that she live at the Reformatory. After a year she graciously bowed out. Her work with the Red Cross was, in any case, far more important.

The list of early Red Cross involvements is long and impressive. However, certain events were milestones.

The 1888 yellow fever epidemic in Jacksonville, Florida, was one such event. Clara was now sixty-six years old but remained as active as ever. As illness spread throughout Jacksonville, she directed the New Orleans chapter of the Red Cross to begin operations.

Her great mistake was in permitting the chapter itself to choose nurses, rather than selecting them herself from the applications she received. Clara assumed that nurses picked in the area would be immune to yellow fever and therefore more suitable to handle the spread of the disease.

What actually happened was that very few truly qualified nurses streamed into Jacksonville. The man placed in charge of the expedition, Colonel F.R. South-mayd, was hasty in his choice of nurses. As a result, a few of his nurses were deemed unsuitable. Some stole Red Cross funds for their own use and committed other acts of misconduct.

The story found its way into several influential newspapers, which horrified Clara. She had trusted the colonel to perform operations as she herself would perform them, thoroughly, carefully, and prudently. Instead, she found the name of the Red Cross sullied and her own judgment in appointing him questioned. Naturally, the unfortunate behavior of the nurses was limited to a very few. Just as naturally, the papers reported the incidents as though they were widespread and commonplace.

Clara was determined that such embarrassments would never happen again. In fact, the following year she had a chance to prove the worthiness of the organization by aiding victims of the historic flood in Johnstown, Pennsylvania. Heavy spring rains contributed to

Evidence of the brutal force of nature unleashed by the devastating flood that destroyed Johnstown, Pennsylvania in May 1889. Nearly three thousand people were killed, and countless homes were washed away by the towering wall of water. Within five days of the disaster, Clara Barton was on the scene, organizing relief efforts, and directing the desperately needed services of the American Red Cross.

the breaking of a dam nearby. A wall of water, usually held back by the dam, flashed through the town, killing three thousand people and countless animals, destroying everything in its path. Here indeed was a chance for the Red Cross to come to the rescue.

Clara was on the scene herself within five days of the tragedy. She never forgot her first walk around the site. Trees and landmarks were uprooted, bodies floating in murky water, houses broken apart, victims staring dazed at what little they had left.

There was also an onslaught of people who called themselves rescue workers. Some were simply interested in watching the proceedings like tourists. Others were professional thieves who were there simply to rob bodies and steal what the living had saved. The police issued statements ordering out anyone who was not there expressly to aid the sufferers.

Clara and her Red Cross workers were viewed skeptically by the Pennsylvania Militia officer in charge. He had never heard of the organization and was at first suspicious. But Clara, remembering the disaster at Jacksonville the year before, had brought with her fifty of the best workers she could round up. In cooperation with the militia, they raised temporary shelters for the homeless and fed, clothed and comforted the victims. Five months later, the worst of the wreckage had been carted away. Schools, stores, and churches were functioning. By November, the last of the Red Cross workers had gone home.

To Clara's extreme disappointment, the triumphant work done by her group was ignored by the press. She had hoped to achieve some recognition for the hard, unrelenting months her workers had spent rebuilding the devastated area. It was only fair, Clara felt, that if they were attacked in the press for their bad behavior that they be applauded when they worked so hard. The silence upset her. As usual for her, Clara's reaction was to work even harder.

At the end of 1891, an international crisis developed that Clara could not ignore. In Russia, the grain harvest, needed to feed millions of people, failed completely. The result was famine throughout that huge country and a desperate need of assistance. Clara had hesitated to involve her organization in situations outside the United States. Now, however, popular opinion was calling for the Red Cross to distribute the food and supplies being collected all over America to help the Russians.

Clara coordinated a gigantic effort to secure and outfit a ship sailing to Russia loaded with tons of food. Julian Hubbell, by this time a qualified doctor, sailed with the ship to act as distributor. He reported to Clara that the joy and thankfulness of the Russian people was almost more than words could describe. For one month in 1892, it is estimated the American Red Cross fed seven hundred thousand people.

The proudest of the relief efforts, however, was undoubtedly the Red Cross work in 1893 at the Sea Islands, a tiny cluster of islands off the coast of South Carolina. The Sea Island residents, mostly poor and black, had been devastated by a hurricane. At first it was believed that no one had survived. Then word began to spread that there were, indeed, a number of hardy people left, and they needed help.

Now seventy-two, Clara was beginning to tire and a

little reluctant to start such a major operation. However, the blacks of the Sea Islands were receiving no other aid from any source, mostly because of their race. Clara knew she had to bring whatever relief she could manage.

With a treasury that was nearly empty and her own funds dangerously low, Clara nonetheless brought in a band of rescue workers and everything she could round up in the way of provisions. The greatest danger lay in the crops that had been ruined by the hurricane. The population had to be kept alive and fed for an entire year, until the next crop could be planted and harvested. How, with almost no money, were they going to do it?

Clara and her group worked harder than they ever had before, teaching the Sea Islands residents new methods of farming, distributing food and clothing, and particularly in helping revive the spirit of the tired people. They insisted that the residents work for their meals, rather than being permitted simply to take what was offered. Willingly, the residents pitched in to help the rebuilding effort. At the end of the year, when the new crop was harvested, Clara and her workers looked around at what they had done. Miraculously, they had kept alive thirty thousand people for an entire year. It was an effort that any organization — particularly one so small and financially unstable — could be proud of.

Unfortunately, all was not rosy in the Red Cross circle. Clara now came under criticism for her methods of directing the group. She was not a meticulous bookkeeper. Her idea of keeping records was collecting scraps of paper on which items were written down, often sloppily and without sufficient information. There was no organized system of accounting, which angered members of the Red Cross Board of Directors, who oversaw all the Red Cross chapters around the world. They felt Clara was either too careless in her work or too arrogant. Perhaps, they suggested, she handled the work this way because she felt she was too important to be questioned.

Actually, these bookkeeping habits rose out of Clara's streak of independence, which had been nurtured since her girlhood. In times of disaster, she was accustomed to giving emergency orders, not taking them. Others who might be more painstaking in setting down records could not match her swiftness in helping those in need. Clara's first thought was always to correct the problem first. She could not be bothered answering to others who wanted to see her methods written down and standardized. Clara was too busy saving lives to back up her methods with paperwork. Now she found herself attacked viciously for this very trait. It was time to set the record straight.

For the first time in her life, Clara spoke out on her own behalf. Through the years she had accepted personal criticism in silence, though it always hurt her. Now she demanded that the Board show its faith in her. She was the founder and main supporter of an organization whose work would never have been done but for her. No one else could possibly have sustained the group during the struggle to exist and then to survive disaster after disaster. She was neither too careless nor too old to handle the office of the Red Cross presidency.

It was a battle Clara ultimately won. The majority of

Clara Barton's improvised Red Cross headquarters in Johnstown, Pennsylvania. While helping survivors of the historic flood, she set up her office in a warehouse, using packing crates as desks and chairs. Over the years the Red Cross flag, pictured here hanging in the corner, has become an international symbol of emergency relief and the care of the ill and suffering.

the Board of Directors agreed with her assessment of her work. They voted her president of the Red Cross for life.

That vote of confidence, denied Clara for most of her life, was just the boost she needed. She knew that she was not as young as she once had been, and that the time was rapidly approaching when she would have to pass some responsibility on to someone stronger. Still, her pride was wounded at the very idea of someone else removing her from office. She wanted her resignation to be her own decision.

It was. In May, 1904, at the age of eighty-two, Clara resigned the presidency of the Red Cross. It was a painful decision, but she knew it was the right one. After twenty-two years, it was time for someone else to shoulder the burden. It was time for Clara to put her affairs in order. It was time to begin wrapping things up.

13

The Final Years

AS CLARA MOVED through her eighties, her interest in the world remained as sharp as ever. Freed from exhausting years of battles with members of the Red Cross, she could concentrate on projects she had thought of for some time but never been able to actually do. She wrote a history of the Red Cross, titled simply "The Red Cross". It was a huge, sprawling, unfocused book seven hundred pages long. Clara herself realized it was haphazard and disorganized, but she was anxious to leave behind a written record of the work done in the years of her supervision.

By now the Red Cross had acquired a headquarters in Glen Echo, Maryland. As a gesture to Clara's leadership, the Board of Directors voted her permanent residency at Glen Echo. So it was there, surrounded by memorabilia of her earlier years, that Clara set about putting her affairs in order.

Her last eight years were a whirlwind of travel to Europe and visits throughout the United States to lecture. She spoke on many topics, always touching on the Red

Cross, the need for preparation and instruction in first aid, and pleas for donations in times of emergency. As always, she was a popular speaker and sought after by many people to attend banquets and functions, where she was often the honored guest. At the same time, she was quietly drawing up a will. She realized her time was growing short.

At the age of ninety Clara caught pneumonia. However, Dr. Hubbell stayed faithfully by her side to nurse her. The following year, however, she contracted double pneumonia. She had no strength left to combat the illness.

Dr. Hubbell and one of her cousins were with her on April 12, 1912. Clara was tossing in bed, delirious. She believed she was back on the battlefields of the Civil War. As her friends struggled to restrain her, she threw off their hands.

"Let me go!" she cried out. "Let me go!"

A moment later she sank back on the sheets. Clara Barton's long, productive life was finally over.

Clara's lifetime was a monument to service. From her earliest childhood days as a nurse to her brother, to her final years as a representative of the American Red Cross, she devoted her time to helping others in every possible way. As a teacher, as a nurse, as a relief worker, her achievements are unparalleled. No other American man or woman has ever given so much in the service of others.

Clara is also unique in that the battles she fought throughout her life were always totally without self-interest. Until the last years of her Red Cross service, she never raised her hand in her own defense, no matter what was said about her or how much it may have hurt. Clara was more interested in securing justice for other people. To that end she bent her amazing dedication to achievements that continue to benefit others to this day.

Every American from Clara's time forward can be grateful to Clara Barton for her contributions. Without her, the simple, practical methods of emergency relief that we have all come to count on might never even have happened. The same young girl who quietly nursed her brother back to health went on to form and lead a national organization ready to provide aid to those in need anywhere at a moment's notice. Thanks to her work, teaching, and inspiration, countless lives have been, and will continue to be, saved around the world.

Other books you might enjoy reading

In alphabetical order:

1. Boylston, Helen Dore. *Clara Barton: Founder of the American Red Cross*. Scholastic Book Services, 1955.

2. Fishwick, Marshall W. and the Editors of Silver Burdett. *Illustrious Americans: Clara Barton*. Silver Burdett Company, 1966.

3. Nolan, Jeannette Covert. *The Story of Clara Barton of the Red Cross*. Julian Messner, 1941.

4. Pryor, Elizabeth Brown. *Clara Barton: Professional Angel*. University of Pennsylvania Press, 1987.

5. Ross, Ishbel. *Angel of the Battlefield: The Life of Clara Barton*. Harper & Brothers Company, 1956.

SUSAN SLOATE has written young-adult fiction, as well as other *Great Lives* books on Abraham Lincoln and Amelia Earhart. She also regularly contributes sports interviews to *Baseball Card News,* a collectors' publication. In her spare time, she rides horses, pilots airplanes, and rafts the California rivers.